Dedication

For my mother, Lilien, who showed me the way to Cape Cod.

Upper reaches of the Herring River, Harwich

Adventure Kayaking

Trips on Cape Cod

Includes Cape Cod National Seashore

David Weintraub

Foreword by Robert Finch

WILDERNESS PRESS
BERKELEY

Library of Congress Card Number 00-020216
ISBN 0-89997-251-9

Manufactured in the United States of America
Published by: **Wilderness Press**
1200 5th Street
Berkeley, CA 94710
(800) 443-7227; FAX (510) 558-1696
mail@wildernesspress.com
www.wildernesspress.com

Contact us for a free catalog

Front cover: Beach at Sandy Neck, Barnstable (Trip 1)
Back cover: *top:* Salt-spray rose
  bottom: Kayaker in Duck Creek, Wellfleet (Trip 21)

Printed on recycled paper, 20% post-consumer waste

Library of Congress Cataloging-in-Publication Data

Weintraub, David, 1949–
    Adventure kayaking : trips on Cape Cod : includes Cape Cod National Seashore / David
Weintraub ; foreword by Robert Finch.
        p. cm.
    Includes bibliographical references (p.) and index.
    ISBN 0-89997-251-9 (alk. paper)
    1. Kayak touring—Massachusetts—Cape Cod—Guidebooks. 2. Cape Cod
(Mass.)—Guidebooks. I. Title.
GV776.M42 C366 2000
917.44'920444—dc21
                                                                                00-020216

Table of Contents

Acknowledgments

I am deeply indebted to Bob Prescott and Dennis Murley of the Wellfleet Bay Wildlife Sanctuary for their help at two important stages in the life of this guide—its birth and its completion. During the busy month of June, both took time to confer with me, to go over my proposed trip list, and to make valuable suggestions about routes, access points, and the Cape's wonderful natural features that I would see along the way. When the manuscript was completed, they reviewed it and offered corrections and comments. I am also grateful for the help provided by Bill Burke, Dana Eldridge, and Mike Whatley at Cape Cod National Seashore, who took time to review the route descriptions pertaining to their area.

Most of my paddling is done solo, but I did have friends along on a few occasions and I was grateful for their company, so thanks go to Keryn Rush, Paul Stillman, and Susan Stillman. Elaine McIlroy at the Wellfleet Library was kind enough to provide me with a hard-to-find book on the place names of Cape Cod, and I thank her for that. Elaine Perry at the Cape Cod Chamber of Commerce kindly supplied me with general information about the Cape and its resources for visitors. Doing the field work for this guide, I had occasion to visit with kayaking outfitters and guides who offered helpful advice, so thanks go to the good people at Jack's Boat Rental, The Paddler's Shop, and Waquoit Kayak Company. Thanks also to staff at the Waquoit Bay National Estuarine Research Reserve for information about their wonderful area and about camping on Washburn Island. The folks at the Goose Hummock Outdoor Center in Orleans have been very helpful to me over the years, and they also deserve credit for their contribution to the amazing growth in popularity of kayaking on Cape Cod.

To everyone at Wilderness Press, thanks for giving me the opportunity to pursue a project close to my heart.

Finally, I would like to thank Maggi, my wife, for her love and support.

Horseshoe crab and glasswort

Foreword

"How dead would the globe seem...if it were not for these water surfaces!"

Henry David Thoreau

One of the most memorable sights I ever had occurred while flying back from Europe several years ago. Outside my window seat, I caught sight of Cape Cod's unmistakable crooked form staring up at me like a familiar face out of the winter sea. From 30,000 feet the landmass of the Cape appeared not only fragile and vulnerable, but almost immaterial. It looked like a flimsy flag floating on the sea, its tattered fabric torn and punctured with hundreds of ponds, streams, tidal creeks, estuaries, bays and harbors. It seemed like a piece of flotsam, adrift on the limitless ocean, almost more water than land itself.

This fanciful image is underlain by a bedrock of fact, for it is not only Cape Cod's present that is writ on water, but its past and future as well. Frozen water, in the form of the glaciers of the last ice age, were the scenery-makers of this sandy peninsula, and the best guesses of geologists suggest that erosion and rising sea levels will return the Cape to the ocean in some sixty centuries. In the meantime, this place of extraordinary natural beauty and diversity is ours to enjoy and to care for, to explore and understand.

If I were to own only one vessel on Cape Cod, I would without hesitation choose a kayak or a canoe. I have sailed or motored on the larger boats of friends, and enjoyed their range and effortless transportation, but no other vessels are so versatile and flexible, so useful for exploring the Cape's many mysteries. None can get you into so many of the Cape's hidden nooks and crannies, the winding labyrinths of its salt marsh creeks, the swampy backwaters of its ponds, the shallows of its tidal flats. They can be launched almost anywhere, almost anytime. On an unexpectedly calm January day you can, within minutes, be out, alone, on an empty harbor, marsh, or pond. Unlike heavier boats, if a rainless season has dried up the connections between ponds, you can simply pick up your kayak and carry it to the next one. If you get caught on an outgoing tide on one of the Cape's extensive areas of tidal flats, you can just get out and walk, pulling your boat behind you.

Speaking of tides, in these light vessels you are by necessity much more aware, and therefore gain a much greater knowledge of, the Cape's variegated lunar currents. You learn, for example, to time your excursions in places like Dennis' Quivett Creek, Scorton's Sandwich Creek, or Truro's Pamet River, so that you can travel up and down these waterways assisted by the tidal flow (or vice-versa if you are out primarily for cardiovascular exercise). Kayaks and canoes are quiet and keep a low profile, letting you follow more closely the Cape's rich, but often wary, marine and avian inhabitants. My friend, the artist Pat de Groot, is renowned for her pen and ink drawings of cormorants, which she has sketched for many years in Provincetown Harbor in a kayak she custom-altered just for that purpose, giving her a perspective on these birds available in no other venue.

By cutting off our legs from our silhouettes, these vessels seem to make us unrecognizable as humans, and therefore as threats, to much of the Cape's waterfowl. I have learned, for instance, that the best way to see shorebirds up close is to deliberately strand myself at low tide on, say, the west side of North Monomoy Island or the flats of Cape Cod Bay in late August. Then I simply wait for the feeding flocks of migrating sandpipers, plovers, dowitchers, whimbrels, willets and other shorebirds to work their way toward me along the hem of the incoming tide until they are literally only yards away.

In April I have followed imperious ranks of alewives in my canoe up several of the Cape's numerous herring streams. In wet springs I have carried my kayak into large vernal pools, low areas I can walk across dry-shod in summer, gliding silently over the submerged constellations of amphibian egg masses. In June I have explored the green-and-blue labyrinthine channels of the Barnstable Marshes, the Cape's largest salt marsh system, watching the magnificently patterned diamondback terrapins (the northernmost large breeding population of these turtles) sunning themselves on the black mud of the creek beds. At low tide the peat banks and the spartina grasses rose like miniature canyon walls above my head, making me as invisible as the terrapins from land.

In July I have sat at high tide over the flats off Gray's Beach in Yarmouthport, my paddle shipped, as clouds of common terns dove into the waters around me after schools of silvery minnows, panicked up from below by the dark weaving forms of ravenous bluefish in a feeding frenzy. In early autumn, on the maple-leaf covered mill ponds of Brewster, I have been startled by a sudden **smack!** on the water surface behind me, and turned to see the magnificent black-and-white bent-wing form of an osprey rise up with a large white perch twisting in its talons. And in November I have kayaked Wellfleet's herring ponds, where the young alewives hatched in the spring and now barely three inches long, line up against the outflow in wavering ranks in the sluiceway between Gull and Higgins ponds, as firmly oriented to the current as the adults that spawned them.

At other times I go out in a harbor, a river, or a pond for no reason other than to experience being on the water in a craft that makes minimal impact on the medium that carries me. At sunset, on a pond whose surface is as still as glass, when mounds of rose-tinted clouds above me are reflected perfectly in the depths below, the only mark on the water is the thin fusiform ripples from the bow of the kayak flowing along its sides like the accordion pleats of a finback whale's throat. In such moments I come as close to the sensation of weightless flying as one can attain on *aqua firma*.

In other words, a kayak or a canoe is a master key to many of Cape Cod's endless natural mysteries. This book shows you some of its more fascinating doors.

Robert Finch
Wellfleet
December 1999

Trip Locator Map

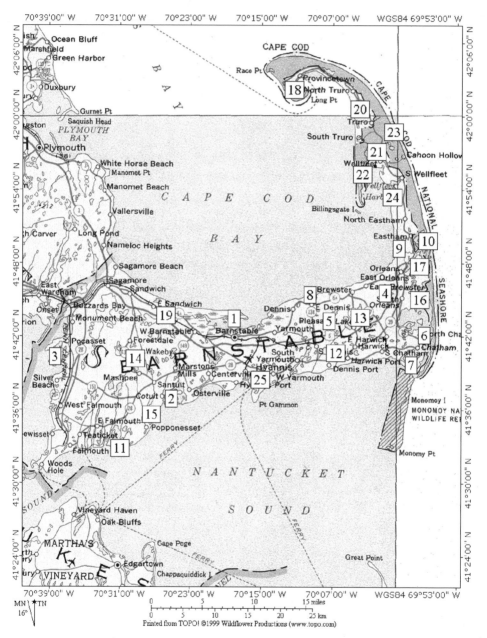

Numbers on this map refer to trips listed in the Table of Contents

Introduction

Cape Cod

The Cape is a paddler's paradise. With a landmass of just under 400 square miles, this "bared and bended arm of Massachusetts," as Thoreau called it, has 560 miles of shoreline, hundreds of freshwater ponds, and numerous bays, harbors, rivers, creeks, and salt marshes to enjoy. Most of the paddling is in these protected waterways, but adventurous kayakers also have the open waters of the Atlantic Ocean, Cape Cod Bay, Buzzards Bay, Nantucket Sound, and Vineyard Sound to explore. Needless to say, the 25 routes described here are merely a sampling of the many possibilities. Cape Cod National Seashore, established in 1961, covers 40 miles of beaches, dunes, forests, ponds, and marshes between Chatham and Provincetown, and offers some of the best paddling on the Cape.

There are 15 towns on the Cape, and many have more than one village within their boundaries. The largest village, Hyannis, is in the town of Barnstable, which is also the name of the county that encompasses the Cape. For the purposes of this guide, the Cape ends at the Cape Cod Canal, but geographically many people (and maps) consider Wareham and Plymouth, towns north of the canal, as part of the Cape. Routes 6, 6A, and 28 connect the towns, so you really can "get there from here," although it may be at a snail's pace during July and August. A location on the Cape is often described in terms of its distance from Boston—somewhere on the upper Cape is closer to Boston than somewhere on the lower Cape, also called the outer Cape. This often goes against common sense—why is Provincetown "lower" than Falmouth? But like so much else here you must take this designation with a grain of salt, and we have plenty of those.

Geology

The foundation of Cape Cod was laid during the Pleistocene Epoch, about 25,000 years ago, when the great ice sheet that covered North America, the Laurentide glacier, pushed south from Canada carrying on its leading edge soil and rocks that eventually formed moraines—walls of glacial debris. The moraines that underlie part of the Cape run northeast through the Elizabeth Islands, then north along the east side of Buzzards Bay, and then turn southeast and finally east, tracing the shore of Cape Cod Bay about half way to the Atlantic shore. In addition to these morainal foundations, the Cape is covered by outwash plains formed when meltwater poured out of the glaciers carrying and then depositing sand, gravel, and boulders. The Cape's many ponds were created when various large blocks of ice that were surrounded by this detritus later melted, leaving depressions in the outwash plain that filled with water. The ponds here are called kettle ponds, and a salt pond is a kettle pond that has an opening to saltwater.

Other features of the landscape—sea cliffs, beaches, barrier islands, salt marshes, and dunes—were created from the glacial raw materials by wind and waves. The sea cliffs that rise more than 150 feet above the Atlantic shore between Wellfleet and Truro were eroded from an outwash plain when sea level rose about 6,000 years ago. The Cape's ever-changing beaches are rearranged yearly by storms that generate pounding surf. The action of the waves combined with currents running parallel to the shore move sand lengthwise along the beach, a process called shore drifting. This creates elongated barriers—islands, beaches, and spits—that protect the water behind them from the action of the surf. The calm water in bays and estuaries behind

Glacial boulder at Cliff Pond

such barriers provides ideal conditions for the creation of salt marshes. Salt-tolerant plants growing in protected waters trap sediments that eventually raise the elevation of a marsh to sea level, where it is cut through by tidal creeks. The low areas of a marsh are flooded twice daily by the tides, but its upper reaches are drowned only during the month's highest tides. Coastal dunes usually form atop barriers and sea cliffs when sand picked up by the wind is deposited there.

Climate and Weather

Paddling season on the Cape generally runs from May through October. Spring, depending on when it arrives, brings a steady and fairly rapid rise in air temperature but a slower rise in water temperature, so the weather can be variable, changing daily, with frequent fog. June is a gorgeous month, when the Cape is in bloom and blue skies usually abound, but rain and cool temperatures are still possible. Blessed with plenty of sunshine and warm temperatures, July and August are the months when most people visit the Cape, crowding beaches and roadways. The summer weather pattern—hazy, hot, and humid—sometimes builds to a heat wave, with daytime temperatures soaring into the 90s. During this time the wind is generally from the southwest, increasing in speed during the afternoon, then dying around dusk. When a front moves through, usually with thunder, lightning, and heavy rain, it breaks the heat wave, sends the wind around to the north, and ushers in several days of cooler and much clearer weather. After Labor Day most of the summer people depart, but this is when the Cape is at its finest, with warm, crystal-clear days and chilly nights redolent with wood smoke. Winter brings wind, rain, and sometimes snow, but also cold, clear days as well.

Average temperatures on the Cape range from a high of 40 degrees and a low of 25 in January to a high of 78 and a low of 63 in July. From June through September the average high is 70 degrees or above. Hurricane season, which runs from late summer through early fall, sometimes brings to the Cape destructive wind, rain, and flooding caused by tidal surges. Winter storms, called northeasters, often produce these same effects, and, like hurricanes, can radically reshape the landscape. Electrical storms usually occur in summer during hot and humid weather. The wind and lightning that accompany these storms can be extremely dangerous. The best source of up-to-the-minute weather information is the recorded broadcasts produced by the National Oceanic and Atmospheric Administration (NOAA). These can be listened to on inexpensive weather radios available at Radio Shack and other dealers. The broadcast for Cape Cod includes information, advisories, watches, and warnings for the adjacent waters.

Tides and Currents

The Cape's tides are a source of wonder and sometimes mystification to visitors. Bays and harbors that are full of water at high tide may be exposed mudflats six hours later. The amount of tidal rise and fall varies over the course of a month, and it is greatest around the time of the new and full moons. The tides having the greatest range are called spring tides, those having the least range, neap tides. Because the Cape is surrounded by six different bodies of water—the Atlantic Ocean, Cape Cod Bay, Buzzards Bay,

Nantucket Sound, Vineyard Sound, and the Cape Cod Canal—keeping track of the tides takes some doing. The easiest way is to get the daily newspaper, *The Cape Cod Times*, and check its tide chart. *The Cape Codder*, a bi-weekly newspaper, publishes a tide chart for the coming week on Fridays. The greatest rise in elevation from low to high tide, almost 10 feet, occurs in Cape Cod Bay. The Atlantic shore sees about a 5-foot rise, Buzzards Bay about 4 feet, and Nantucket Sound about 2.5 feet.

The Cape's tides are very regular, advancing about 50 minutes every 24 hours. For example, a noon high tide would be followed the next day by a high tide at 12:50 P.M. The outer Cape's Atlantic beaches—Provincetown, Truro, Wellfleet, Eastham—reach high tide within a few minutes of each other. Orleans and Chatham lag behind by about 15 minutes. On Cape Cod Bay high tide occurs for all the towns at about the same time and is within a few minutes of high tide along the outer Cape's Atlantic beaches. Nantucket Sound lags behind Cape Cod Bay by about 45 minutes. The farther a bay, harbor, river, creek, or marsh is from the source of its tidewater, the longer it will take to fill. Because many of the routes in this guide explore such waterways, I have calculated the best time for you to start these routes based on high tide for the nearest point covered by the tide table. For example, Nauset Marsh takes several hours to fill, so I recommend launching at the time of high tide for Nauset Beach, Orleans. This will ensure that your tour of the marsh will take place around the time of *its* high tide.

Wherever one body of water joins another, a possibility for strong currents exists. This is especially true where the tide forces water through a narrow opening such as an inlet, or where water swirls around the tip of a barrier spit. For most of the trips covered by this guide, currents are not an issue. There are a few trips, however, where the potential for strong currents exists. I have noted these situations in the route descriptions and in the section s preceeding them called "Tips" (see below).

Plant Communities

In *Common Trailside Plants of Cape Cod National Seashore*, Michael E. Whatley divides the Cape's plant communities as follows:

Impoverished sandy soil, dunes, heathlands. Here you may find such hearty plants as beach grass, dusty miller, broom crowberry, poverty grass, beach pea, and scrub oak.

Upland forests, dry and open woods. These are mixed forests of pitch pine, black oak, white oak, black cherry, and sassafras, with an understory of bearberry and black huckleberry.

left to right: pickerelweed; poison ivy; saltwater cordgrass

Moist lowland woods, developed forests. American beech, tupelo, blueberry, sweet pepperbush, and swamp azalea characterize these areas, along with winterberry, shadbush, inkberry, and sheep laurel.

Freshwater ponds, streams. Look here for pickerelweed, white water lily, meadowsweet, military rushes, and slender arrowhead. The Cape's freshwater sandy beaches have many rare plants, most notably Plymouth gentian.

Freshwater swamps, receding ponds, shallow bogs. Within the national seashore you will find a red-maple swamp and an Atlantic white-cedar swamp, both worth visiting.

Back dunes, transitional fields. Beach plum, bayberry, salt-spray rose, blackberry, and poison ivy are found throughout the Cape in these habitats.

Open fields, forest margins. Stands of eastern red cedar, along with vines such as Virginia creeper and fox grape, characterize these areas.

Altered, previously cultivated habitats. Black locust, a fast-growing tree, has been planted extensively on the Cape, but its shallow roots make it unstable in high winds.

Saltwater marshes. These important ecosystems are characterized by salt-tolerant plants such as saltwater cordgrass, salt hay, glasswort, and sea lavender.

Birds

Most of the animals you will see from your kayak will be birds, and Cape Cod is one of the finest places in the world to view them. The Cape Cod Bird Club checklist contains more than 300 species, including many local nesters. Among the nesting species you may see are piping plover, listed as threat-

Yellow-crowned night-heron

ened under federal law, least tern, common tern, great black-backed gull, herring gull, laughing gull, osprey, willet, American oystercatcher, mute swan, Canada goose, belted kingfisher, redwinged blackbird, and green heron. During spring and fall, the Cape's bird population surges dramatically as waves upon waves of migrants descend on its marshes, fields, and woodlands to feed and rest. In the months of May and September, more than 30 species of shorebirds have been recorded on the Cape, and for those months about the same number of warbler species have been tallied. In summer, about half a dozen species of gulls and terns are commonly seen and the total number of species recorded is more than 20. In winter, ice-free waters on the Cape are home to ducks and geese, and the number of these species recorded in the month of December is more than 30.

Human History

Although the name "Cape Cod" was bestowed in 1602 by an English explorer, Bartholomew Gosnold, many of the Cape's names speak of its Native American heritage as the land of the Wampanoags—Mashpee, Nauset, and Pamet are a few examples. It is believed that native people first came here around 9,000 years ago, and that by 800 years ago they had developed agriculture and were using fire as a forest-management technique. By the time of Samuel de Champlain's visits in 1605 and 1606, the Wampanoags had six villages from Chatham to Wellfleet, were living in domed shelters thatched with grasses, reeds, and bark, and were growing corn, beans, squash, and tobacco. In November 1620, after a 65-day crossing, the *Mayflower* sailed north along the outer shore, rounded Provincetown's hooked tip, and made safe harbor behind its protective arm. The Pilgrims, led by Capt. Myles Standish, made three exploratory trips around Cape Cod Bay in a small boat, or shallop, finally deciding on Plymouth as the place of settlement.

For a few decades after the Pilgrims left the Cape, things were as they had been before their arrival. But some in Plymouth eventually returned to settle on the Cape, and soon they were cutting its forests to clear land for agriculture and livestock and to obtain timber for homes, boats and fuel. The land could not support this overuse and began to erode into desert. This change forced the settlers to seek their livelihoods elsewhere, and the sea was the obvious choice. By the 1700s, Cape fishermen were plying the near-shore waters and sailing as far as the Grand Banks off Newfoundland in search of cod. By the mid-1800s, Provincetown boasted a fleet of more than 100 cod trawlers and 200 mackerel schooners, and other towns had substantial, if smaller, fleets of their own.

Seamanship was a way of life, and Cape sailors made names for themselves as captains of trans-oceanic clipper ships in the mid-1800s. The town of Brewster is said to have been home to 50 sea captains during this time. Packet boats running between New York, Boston, and the Cape brought mail, passengers, salt, and other cargo to and fro. Whaling also played an important role in early Cape life, and the towns of Wellfleet and Provincetown were whaling ports before New Bedford and Nantucket rose to fame. The waters off Cape Cod are some of the most treacherous in the world, and an estimated 3,000 vessels have perished on the Atlantic coast there. Beginning in 1797, a number of lighthouses were erected on Cape soil to warn mariners of its deadly bars and shoals. In 1872, Congress established the US Life Saving Service, which eventually become the Coast Guard, and stations were set up all along the Cape. The opening of the Cape Cod Canal in 1914, linking Buzzards Bay and Cape Cod Bay, greatly reduced the number of wrecks and loss of life.

The Cape suffered an economic decline after the Civil War, but the coming of the railroad, which reached all the way to Provincetown by 1873, helped matters considerably. Soon the well-to-do from elsewhere were building summer homes on Buzzards Bay and Nantucket Sound, hunters from New York and Boston were flocking to the bays and marshes to shoot waterfowl and shorebirds, and a community of artists and writers was coalescing around Provincetown and eventually would include major figures in American cultural life. After World War I the Cape became more accessible for weekend visitors, and after World War II its popularity as a vacation spot soared. In 1961, President Kennedy signed legislation creating Cape Cod National Seashore, which protects from development 28,000 acres of beaches, dunes, forests, marshes, and ponds. Today the Cape is enjoyed by visitors from all over the world who come to revel in its natural beauty and share in its wonderful history. (Much of the above information is from the official Cape Cod National Seashore guide, written by Robert Finch.)

Using This Guidebook

Selecting a Route

Many kayaking guides include a rating system that attempts to tell readers whether they will find a particular route easy or difficult. After much thought I decided not to include such a system, and here's why. Nearly all the trips herein can be handled by a novice paddler in relatively good shape, provided the conditions are favorable. And conversely, many of the trips would challenge even experienced paddlers, given poor conditions. So what would I be rating, the route or the conditions? I have opted instead to give at the beginning of each route description its length in miles and a snapshot of what the trip entails (see below). This said, here are some guidelines for matching a route with your ability and your inclination.

The longest route I describe in this guide is about 9 miles, the shortest just under 2. Going over the notes I made at the time, I find I completed the 9-mile trip in 4.5 hours and the 2-mile trip in 1 hour. These times include poking around to look at birds and plants, stopping to check the map, drifting while I shot photographs, and going ashore for lunch. My normal paddling rate seems to be about 2 miles per hour regardless of whether the trip is long or short. Beating into the wind on the return leg of an out-and-back route slowed me down to about 1.5 miles per hour. On another day however, when an electrical storm threatened, I paddled considerably faster, about 3 miles per hour. The point is, as you gain experience as a paddler, you will probably be able to judge how long a given route will take you to complete.

But distance isn't everything. Over the years I have found wind to be the most important factor in determining the kind of experience I have on the water, making the difference between an enjoyable paddle and an ordeal of endurance. Wind speed and direction are both important. A light breeze coming across your bow may be cool and refreshing, but a stiff one blowing from the same direction may make it seem as if you were paddling uphill. Wind coming from the side, or abeam, may make it difficult for you to hold your course, unless you have a rudder. And wind coming from behind may be accompanied by following seas, which tend to cause your kayak to broach, or turn sideways to the waves, another situation in which a rudder helps.

If the trip takes you through saltwater, tide will be a factor. Because the Cape experiences a dramatic rise and fall of the tides, its bays, harbors, and creeks that are flooded at noon may be empty by 6 P.M. In most cases, saltwater trips are best started a few hours before high tide and completed a few hours after. For these trips I have noted the best time to launch under "Tips." If this time is inconvenient for you, there are freshwater trips to select from, where tide is not a factor. Finally, if you are paddling with a group and have been chosen as the leader, please consider the abilities of all members of your party. No one enjoys being left behind and having to struggle to catch up.

Route Descriptions

At their most basic, the route descriptions in this guide are designed at least to get you safely from the launch site to a particular point and back again. Hopefully they will do more than just that. I have tried to provide you with information designed to make your paddle trip enjoyable and educational. Simply put, I love Cape Cod and I want to share the best parts of it with you. Among the things that make the Cape a special place for me are its history, its plant and bird life, and the wonderful variety of its waterways—from the open expanse of Cape Cod Bay, to the salt marshes and tidal creeks, to the hidden freshwater kettle ponds deep in the pines. So along the way, in addition to giving the directional headings and noting features of the landscape, I describe a bird or two here, a native tree or shrub there. When something from the Cape's history seems appropriate, I offer it as well. Additionally, each route description is preceded by information, flagged by bold-face headings, to help you easily find all the things you may want to know *before* setting out.

Length. Length tells you how many miles of paddling the route as described covers. If you know your per-mile paddling rate, you can figure the time it will take to complete the route. Because paddling rate varies so much from person to person, and also depends on conditions, I made no attempt to calculate the time each trip would take. Many of the trips described lend themselves to further exploration or lounging on the beach and thus even a relatively short route can easily be turned into an all-day excursion.

Highlights. This is a snapshot version of the trip, showing you at a glance the route and some of the special things you will see along the way.

Nearby attractions. Before or after your paddle you will probably want to visit nearby areas of scenic and historical interest. Some of the most popular are listed here, with their locations and, where appropriate, phone numbers for more information. To fully take advantage of all the Cape has to offer, I recommend Kim Grant's excellent book, *Cape Cod, Martha's Vineyard & Nantucket: An Explorer's Guide.*

Tips. Look here for information about when in the tide cycle to launch, what to bring on board with you, and other advice to make your trip more enjoyable.

Directions. For all but one trip, driving directions to the launch site are given from Rt. 6, the Cape's main highway. For Trip 7 in Chatham, driving directions are given from the Rt. 28 rotary. For Trips 6, 12, and 17, which are

Kayak atop car on home-made carrier

shuttle trips, directions are given first to the landing site and then to the launch.

Parking and facilities. Unless otherwise indicated, all parking areas described in this guide are free and open to the general public. Several of the trips in this guide start at state-run boat ramps where a small fee is charged during summer. A few trips launch from beaches or landings that are served by parking areas where a resident beach sticker is required during summer, usually from the last weekend in June through Labor Day. All parking restrictions and fees are noted. If you are renting a house on the Cape, check with the property owner to see if a guest permit is available. I have listed facilities such as toilets, phones, and other amenities available in the parking area or nearby, but keep in mind that some of these may be seasonal and therefore unavailable when you visit.

Launch. Getting your boat safely in the water is the goal, and where there is a boat ramp that may be crowded with powerboats I have tried to provide an alternative, which usually involves carrying your boat. If you are solo this may not be an option, so try to have everything ready before you drive down the ramp, and be prepared to launch quickly and move out of the way of other boats. Otherwise, all launches are from beaches or shores.

Safety

You already own and have with you at all times the most important piece of safety equipment—your brain. Most boating accidents happen as a result of poor judgment. Many factors contribute to poor judgment, but perhaps the most important is overestimating your abilities or the abilities of those around you. Other factors that can impair judgment include fatigue, hunger, dehydration, heat, and cold. There is no substitute for experience—hours spent on the water—but it is certainly a good idea to enroll in a kayaking class or clinic. There you will learn basic self-rescue and group-rescue techniques, how to read the water, the wind, and the weather, and also how to become a more efficient paddler, expending less energy per stroke. All these will contribute to your enjoyment and safety.

Equipment

Kayak. Sea kayaks, or touring kayaks as they are also known, come in two basic styles—open and closed deck. Open-deck boats resemble bulky surfboards with raised sides. Closed-deck boats have an opening, or cockpit, in which you sit. In both styles of boat, your back should be comfortably supported and your legs somewhat flexed. Most boats have foot rests or steering pedals that can be adjusted to provide the best leg position. The advantage of an open-deck boat is ease of use—to get started you just hop on and start paddling. If you fall off you can just climb back on. Some people dislike having their legs enclosed beneath a deck, and for them an open-deck boat is the only choice. A closed-deck boat offers much more protection from the elements— sun, wind, water—and is more stable because your center of gravity is below the waterline.

Kayaks in the stores today are made from a variety of materials, including plastic, Kevlar, and fiberglass. For typical paddlers who don't want to spend time worrying about the upkeep of their boats, and who also don't want to be afraid to bang them around a bit, plastic is probably the best choice. Boats come in many different lengths and widths, with seating for one—called a single—or two people, called a double. Doubles are fine for people whose paddling styles are well matched and who will always have partners to paddle with, but for most people a single is the best option. Unless you are going to haul two weeks' worth of gear to remote campsites, you don't need a behemoth. Remember, you are going to have to get the boat on and off your car and to and from the launch site. Are you always going to have a partner to help? If not, size and weight are issues to consider. In addition, a shorter boat is usually easier to turn than a longer one, but unless fitted with a rudder it probably won't track as straight.

One feature to look at carefully is a boat's stability, usually defined in terms of initial and secondary characteristics. Initial stability is the way the boat feels when you first get in; secondary stability is how the boat behaves when you begin to lean it on its side. For example, a wide, flat-bottomed kayak feels stable at first but becomes less stable as you lean it, and eventually it flips over. A sleek touring craft, on the other hand, feels tippy at first but actually gets more stable as you lean it. Secondary stability is important because it helps the boat resist capsizing. Also, there are maneuvers you may want to learn for turning and bracing that involve leaning your boat.

When choosing a kayak, comfort is the top priority. All the performance features in the world won't help if your derriere hurts after 30 minutes of paddling. Because people come in different shapes and sizes, the only way to tell if a boat fits is to spend time in it. You can do this by renting before you buy, and also by attending demo days offered by kayaking shops. If you try as many different styles and designs as you can, you'll begin to learn what to look for when it comes time to buy. Among the bells and whistles to consider are a rudder, useful for turning but also for keeping the boat tracking straight when the wind and seas are from the side or behind; compartments below deck for stowing gear; and an ample supply of elastic shock cords, called deck bungees, stretched across the deck in front of and behind the cockpit. Above all, make sure you are dealing with a knowledgeable salesperson and a reliable store.

Paddle. This is an area of personal preference: either you prefer the feel of wood to plastic or you don't. Either kind will get the job done, and wood does require maintenance. Other choices are length and blade shape, which depend on your height, how long your arms are, the width of your boat, what kind of paddling stroke you have, and the type of conditions you typically encounter. Make sure whatever paddle you use has the ability to adjust the angle of feathering, which is the orientation of the blades with respect to each other. Feathering helps the out-of-water blade cut through the air with minimum resistance, but requires some getting used to as you paddle. Most useful, I believe, are paddles that have three positions: zero degrees, 90 degrees, and somewhere in between, say 60 degrees. Finally, use a paddle leash—a nylon or elastic cord attached to a deck bungee—to keep from losing your paddle.

Personal floatation device (PFD). Life jackets, or PFDs, should be worn by every person in a kayak. If you find yourself in the water and incapacitated, a type-III PFD will keep you afloat on your back with your nose and mouth out of the water. Buy a life jacket specially designed for wearing in a kayak—these offer the best comfort and freedom of movement. Make sure the jacket fits snugly and can't ride up over your head. Select one that has convenient pockets and attachment points for safety equipment such as a strobe light and a whistle. When wearing your PFD in your boat, secure the zipper and all other fasteners.

Spray skirt. This oval-shaped piece of nylon or neoprene fits snugly around your waist and then fastens over the coaming, or raised lip, that encir-

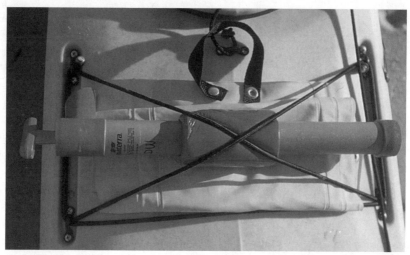

Paddle float and bilge pump on kayak deck

cles the cockpit of your kayak. As its name implies, it is designed to keep water out of the cockpit, but it also provides insulation, keeps out bugs, and offers protection from the sun. On calm water in warm weather its use is optional: some paddlers do without; others fasten it loosely around themselves and leave it attached to the rear, but unattached to the front, of the coaming.

Paddle float. This inflatable bag slips over your paddle blade and allows you to use your paddle as a stabilizing device during a self-rescue. Stow it and your bilge pump under the deck bungees within easy reach.

Bilge pump. If you accidentally tip over and come out of your boat—a happening called a wet exit—the cockpit will fill with water. After you right your boat, stabilize it, and climb back in, a bilge pump allows you to get most of the water out of the cockpit.

Dry bags. These heavy-duty nylon bags feature a roll-top closure that buckles shut and ensures a waterproof seal. They come in many sizes and colors, and there are clear ones as well, so you can see the contents. It is handy to have a small one with safety equipment to keep in your cockpit, and larger ones for camping equipment, clothing, food, and other supplies.

Navigation equipment. For years I paddled without a deck compass, relying instead on my sense of direction and a hand-held compass attached to my life jacket. Now I can't imagine doing without one. It helps me orient my map if I am using one, lets me follow a predetermined course if I have the headings, keeps me paddling straight when there are no landmarks to sight on, and allows me to take bearings on landscape features for later identification. The best deck compass to buy is one that attaches to a mounting plate that in

Kayak deck-mount compass

Kayak foredeck with map in zip-lock bag, compass, water bottle, and GPS

turn clips onto your deck bungees, thus eliminating the need to drill holes in your boat. Even if you carry electronic navigation equipment (see below) you should always have a compass on board for backup.

Global positioning system (GPS) devices have revolutionized navigation and are a boon to boaters, especially when out of sight of land, at night, or in fog. Having one on board your kayak may be useful provided you can keep it on deck where it has a clear view of the sky. You can buy a soft-plastic case, made for cell phones and hand-held GPS units, with a waterproof closure and a nylon cord, that is perfect for this purpose. Use a computer mapping program such as TOPO! to transfer route information, called waypoints, from a PC to your GPS device, and then use the GPS to navigate when you are on the water. If you are doing an out-and-back route, you can mark waypoints on the outbound leg and then follow them on the way back. You can also set the device to record your position automatically at set intervals as you paddle, and then plot your route on your PC when you get home.

Emergency signaling devices. Signaling devices are inexpensive, small, and lightweight, so there is no reason not to carry them. I have a waterproof strobe light and a whistle attached to my life jacket at all times. I also keep signal flares and a small signal horn in a dry bag in the cockpit. A VHF radio or a cell phone (provided there is reception) is useful in emergencies.

Other stuff. Here are some other things that may come in handy and can easily be stored in a dry bag: duct tape, flashlight, batteries, first-aid supplies, knife, sunscreen, insect repellent, snacks, quick-dry towel, and binoculars.

Clothing

Summer paddling on the Cape requires little more than a swimsuit and a shirt to protect you from the sun. Outdoor clothing manufacturers make garments from nylon with a built-in sun block. A long-sleeved shirt made from this quick-drying material is ideal for kayaking in the harsh sun. Hats are also essential for sun protection, and there are many on the market now with wide brims and safari-style neck drapes. For safety I always have on board a lightweight nylon windbreaker and synthetic vest. These can be stored in a dry bag and stowed in a compartment below deck. If the weather is chilly, many paddlers start with a layer of synthetic long underwear—pants and top—and then add outer layers as needed. Wetsuits and waterproof/windproof paddling jackets, hats, and gloves offer the ultimate in protection from cold weather.

Navigation and Maps

I have tried to make the routes described in this guide as easy to follow as possible. To that end I have included four types of aids to keep you from getting lost: landmarks, headings, compass points, and directions (left, right). Landmarks are obvious features, either natural or man-made; most have names and most appear on maps. An example would be "The land on your left now is Barley Neck." I use the term "heading," as in "turn right to a heading of about 80 degrees," to refer to a compass bearing based on magnetic north, which on the Cape is about 16 degrees west of true north. However, because maps are oriented to true rather than magnetic north, when I refer to a direction *on a map* I use true directions, as in "a small inlet reaching south." I use the term "course," as in "Continue paddling on a southward course until you draw near Scraggy Neck," to mean a general direction of travel. The directions "left" and "right" assume you are facing forward in your boat or facing the water if on land. Most of the routes are loops or one-way shuttle trips, but a few are out-and-back trips on which you retrace your route to the launch site. For these you must navigate the return leg using your memory and the book's route description of the outbound leg, or your GPS.

The maps herein are based on the same ones I used during my summer of paddling to gather the information for this guide. Using a PC and a computer mapping program called TOPO! by Wildflower Productions, I printed maps of the areas I wanted to visit and kept them on deck in plastic bags as I paddled. These are USGS maps, which are highly detailed and show both onshore and near-shore features. The biggest advantage to printing your own maps using TOPO! is that you can customize them to fit your selected route, you can plot distance and headings, and you can add other information such as GPS waypoints (see above). There is a very useful nautical chart, printed on waterproof plastic, that covers Pleasant Bay from Orleans to Chatham on one side and Chatham to Monomoy Island on the other—look for it in kayak shops and marine-supply stores.

Protecting the Environment

Camping is generally not allowed on Cape beaches. The one exception in this guide is Washburn Island, described in Trip 11. Many of the beaches described in this guide are nesting areas for terns and shorebirds, including the federally threatened piping plover. During nesting season, generally late spring through midsummer, these areas are roped off and posted with signs explaining the closure. Please obey all signs and closures. Even in areas that are not closed, be careful where you step—shorebird eggs and chicks are colored to blend in with the sand. Follow established paths and avoid trampling vegetation. Freshwater kettle ponds are fragile ecosystems and need to be treated gently—using soap of any kind or watering dogs and other pets can be harmful. Cape Cod National Seashore and the Cape's individual towns have rules designed to protect the environment: please learn and respect them.

Nauset Beach, bird-nesting area

Where to Get More Information

Books and other publications

The best all-purpose guidebook for the Cape is Kim Grant's *Cape Cod, Martha's Vineyard & Nantucket: An Explorer's Guide*, published by The Countryman Press. In it you will find chapters on each of the Cape's towns plus the two neighboring islands. The guide is chock-full of information on how to get around, what to see, where to stay, and where to dine. The index, always a test of a useful guidebook, is superb. The book is illustrated with photographs by the author, a professional photographer, and well-drawn maps.

Other useful guidebooks include *Cape Cod, Its Natural and Cultural History*, Cape Cod National Seashore's official guide by Robert Finch, and *Birding Cape Cod*, by Cape Cod Bird Club and Massachusetts Audubon Society. The Cape Cod Chamber of Commerce publishes *Cape Cod, The Official Guide*, available free, that has information about arts, culture and history, recreation, dining, shopping, transportation, and accommodations. Many of the Cape towns publish their own brochures for visitors. *Canoe & Kayak* magazine is full of tips and techniques to improve your paddling skills, PO Box 3146, Kirkland, WA 98083.

Maps

In addition to the maps you can create yourself using a PC and TOPO!, there are a few other sources of useful maps. The best all-purpose maps for driving around the Cape and getting to the launch sites are in *Cape Cod & Islands Atlas and Guide Book*, published by Butterworth of Cape Cod. The maps clearly mark town landings, making them particularly useful to kayakers and other boaters. In addition to maps, the atlas contains important phone numbers for each town, a description of points of interest, sections on sports and outdoor recreation, and a page on Cape Cod National Seashore.

There is a National Geographic Trails Illustrated topographic map for Cape Cod National Seashore, printed on tear-proof plastic, which covers the area from Provincetown south to Monomoy Island and west to Brewster and Harwich. Much more than just a map, it contains information about the Cape's geology, cultural and natural history, and recreation. BikeMaps Massachusetts publishes a map that covers on one side Cape Cod and the Islands, and on the other Cape Ann and the North Shore (north of Boston). Although geared to cyclists, it is a good, all-purpose locator map for all the trips described in this guide.

Visitor centers

Cape Cod National Seashore has two visitor centers open to the public, with interpretive displays, historical films, an orientation movie, maps, books, guided walks, and helpful staff: **Salt Pond visitor center**, (508) 255-3241, off Rt. 6 in Eastham, open daily 9 A.M. to 4:30 P.M. (extended hours in summer, reduced hours in winter, closed December 25th); **Province Lands visitor center**, (508) 487-1256, Race Point Rd. off Rt. 6 in Provincetown, open daily April–November, 9 A.M. to 4:30 P.M. (extended hours in summer).

Massachusetts Audubon Society operates the **Wellfleet Bay Wildlife Sanctuary**, (508) 349-2615, located in South Wellfleet west of Rt. 6 near West Rd. The visitor center here has interpretive displays, books, maps, and helpful staff.

Cape Cod Chamber of Commerce, (508) 862-0700, and most of the Cape towns have visitor centers or places to get tourism information.

Chapter 1

Barnstable

TRIP 1  **BARNSTABLE HARBOR TO SANDY NECK**

Length: 8 miles

Highlights

This is simply one of the best tours on the Cape. The paddling is richly varied, including open but protected water, tidal creeks, and offshore shallows. The scenery is superb—you will see pristine beaches, rolling dunes, salt marshes, a weather-beaten village, and even an old lighthouse. Ospreys, terns, and shorebirds are among the avian attractions, and you also have a chance to learn about some of the Cape's hearty native plants.

Nearby attractions

Sandy Neck and Great Marshes form a wonderful conservation area consisting of a 4000-acre salt marsh, pine woodlands, rolling dunes, and barrier beach. Access is off Sandy Neck Rd. north of Rt. 6A on the Sandwich/W. Barnstable line. For more information call the Sandy Neck gatehouse, (508) 362-8300, or the Barnstable Dept. of Natural Resources, (508) 790-6272.

Tips

Launch about three hours before high tide for Cape Cod Bay. A whale-watching tour boat departs daily from Barnstable inner harbor April through October. Get a copy of the boat's schedule and stay well out of its way.

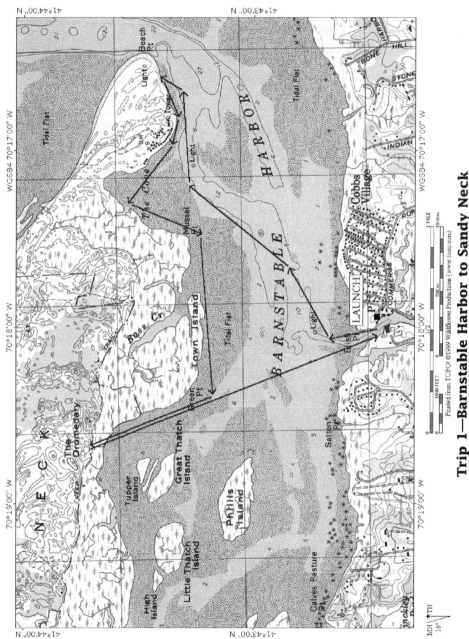

Trip 1—Barnstable Harbor to Sandy Neck

Directions

From Rt. 6 eastbound in Barnstable, take Exit 6, signed for Rt. 132, Barnstable, and Hyannis. After exiting bear left and follow Rt. 132 north for 0.7 mile to a stop sign at Rt. 6A. Turn right and go 2.6 miles to a traffic signal at Mill Way (signed MILLWAY). Turn left and go 0.6 mile to a parking area, left, for the Blish Point boat ramp.

From Rt. 6 westbound in Yarmouth, take Exit 7, signed for Willow St., Yarmouthport, and W. Yarmouth. Turn right onto Willow St. and go 1 mile to Rt. 6A. Turn left and go 2.4 miles to a traffic signal at Mill Way (signed MILL-WAY). Turn right and go 0.6 mile to a parking area, left, for the Blish Point boat ramp.

Parking and facilities

The parking area and boat ramp are operated by the Massachusetts Public Access Board. During summer there is a small fee for parking and boat launching. Use is free during the rest of the year. On summer weekends the lot is usually full by 9 or 10 A.M. There are toilets here.

Launch

Use the boat ramp to unload and then, after parking, launch from the sandy beach just to its north. Or park first and then carry your boat down a set of steps from the parking area to the beach.

Trip Description

A narrow passage connects Barnstable's inner harbor, a small inlet reaching south, with a much larger body of water called Barnstable Harbor to the north. As you launch into this passage, the inner harbor is left and Barnstable Harbor is right. Barnstable Harbor is formed by the eastward-reaching arm of Sandy Neck, which ends at a wide opening to Cape Cod Bay. The harbor is a busy place, with many pleasure craft arriving and departing, and there is also a large whale-watching tour boat that runs daily tours from here April through October, so stay alert. Turning right, you paddle north through the passage and into Barnstable Harbor.

As you round Blish Point, right, you have the main channel, marked by red and green poles protruding from the water, ahead. Keeping the green poles just on your left, you stay out of the busy channel, yet well offshore to avoid submerged rocks and shallows—at half-tide there are only several feet of water outside of the channel. With an incoming tide, you will have a current running against you, which may not be noticeable until you stop paddling and begin to drift backward. To your right is a lovely stretch of beach and a community shown on the USGS map as Cobbs Village. The set of channel markers you are following ends with a piling topped by a light. Once past it, turn right to a heading of about 80 degrees and paddle toward the center of the harbor, with the vast expanse of Sandy Neck to the north and the wide opening to Cape Cod Bay ahead in the distance.

Soon you reach green can 13, a channel marker on your left. When there is no boat traffic, turn north across the channel and continue paddling toward Sandy Neck, heading for the village and the old lighthouse near its tip. A lighthouse was first erected on Sandy Neck in 1827, four years after one was put up on Billingsgate at the mouth of Wellfleet Harbor. Previous to these, the Cape's first two lighthouses were on the Atlantic shore—Highland Light, also called Cape Cod Light, in Truro (1797) and Race Point Light, in Provincetown (1816). A heading of about 70 degrees will keep you clear of the channel, which is now on your right, and away from the shallows off Mussel Point, left. As you pass The Cove, a triangular indentation wedged north into Sandy Neck, the channel swings close to shore, forcing you left. Powerboats come ripping through here on their way to and from Cape Cod Bay, and you want to give them plenty of room.

Sandy Neck itself is an approximately 6-mile strip of coastal dunes and barrier beach that encloses and helped create the Cape's largest salt marsh, stretching from Sandwich on the west to Dennis on the east. The Great Marshes, as this 4,000-acre wetland is known, once provided a bountiful sup-

Kayaks on the beach at Sandy Neck

Cottages built in the late 19th and early 20th centuries now serve as summer retreats

ply of salt hay (*Spartina patens*) for the early settlers, who used it for fodder. Sandy Neck, like many other sand spits and barrier beaches, was formed by shore drifting, a process whereby water currents carry eroded material parallel to the shoreline and then deposit it in the deeper water commonly found at the mouth of a bay. Once the bay has been partly enclosed and protected, layers of silt begin to accumulate in the still waters, eventually forming mudflats where marsh plants can take root, which in turn trap more silt and raise the elevation of the marsh.

The village of more than 50 weathered wooden shacks near the east tip of Sandy Neck is remarkably isolated—residents travel to and fro by boat or by 4X4 along a jeep trail through the dunes. Some of the gray-shingled homes sit just above the high-tide line, and others are raised on pilings. A few carry names: Sunset, Last Resort. There is no electricity out here, and residents must pump their water from wells. No new construction is allowed. According to a Town of Barnstable brochure, the village here consists of hunting and recreational cottages built during the late 19th and early 20th centuries, now used as summer retreats. The lighthouse, which was decommissioned and sold in the 1930s, still stands guard over the village. Next to the lighthouse is the keeper's cottage, a square building with steeply pitched roof lines and gables on each side. You will see similar cottages if you visit Hardings Beach in Chatham, where the old Stage Harbor Light still stands, or

Wellfleet's Mayo Beach. (On the USGS map, the lighthouse is marked "Tower.")

Now passing the village's waterfront homes and then the lighthouse, you can land on a gently sloping sandy beach near the tip of Sandy Neck. This is wild country out here—just low dunes with clumps of beach grass, open water leading to Cape Cod Bay, and, on a clear day, plenty of blue sky. Here is a perfect spot for a rest stop or a picnic lunch. Be sure to pull your boat well back from the waterline if the tide is rising. When Cape Cod Bay is calm, adventurous kayakers can paddle around the tip of Sandy Neck and explore its north shore, but beware of a strong rip current that can run between the harbor and the bay.

When you are done enjoying this special place, retrace your route along the shoreline and then turn north into The Cove. If it is near high tide, you will find deep water in here, and on The Cove's west side there is a wonderful salt marsh worth exploring. Some of the Cape's common salt-marsh plants, including saltwater cordgrass, glasswort, and sea lavender, are here, and you can paddle through tidal creeks back into the marsh. Continuing a counter-clockwise circuit of The Cove, you turn southwest toward Mussel Point on a heading of about 210 degrees. Near the point is an osprey-nesting platform, one of many in the Cape's marshes. These platforms have been very successful in attracting nesting pairs of ospreys—large, fish-eating hawks that were almost wiped out by DDT. After its use was banned, these magnificent birds, with the help of nesting platforms scattered in marshes throughout the Cape, staged a remarkable comeback.

Remote village and old lighthouse at tip of Sandy Neck

Once around Mussel Point, marked by a piling in the water, you turn right and come to a heading of about 300 degrees. Now you have a low sandy beach on your right, which may be teeming with noisy terns. The next large inlet on your right is Bass Creek, and as you pass it make sure to stay south of Town Island, ahead. Town Island is mostly salt marsh, flooded at high tide. In early summer be on the lookout for striped bass moving in schools through the shallows just offshore. Green Point, on the southwest side of Town Island, also is marked by a piling. As you pass the point, turn right and head for a feature on Sandy Neck called The Dromedary—an area of low dunes with many humps forming the most extensive dunes on the Cape's bay side. A heading of about 340 degrees will take you into a salt marsh just south of The Dromedary, with Town Island on your right. There are several narrow creeks in the marsh, so if you want to land here, find one and paddle as close to shore as you can get. Use caution: at other than peak high tides, you may find yourself several feet below the creek bank, making it hard to exit and re-enter your boat. The silty bottom of some of these creeks resembles quicksand and can easily trap you if you are on foot.

Just back from the marsh is the jeep trail, which floods during extreme high water. To the west, a lone weather-beaten house sits facing the marsh. Above the highest-tide line are eastern red cedar, bayberry, beach plum, salt-spray rose, Virginia creeper, and a ton of poison ivy. When you have finished exploring this wonderful part of Sandy Neck, retrace your route to Green Point. As the tide drops, several islands to your right, Tupper and Great Thatch, begin to show themselves. A heading of due south takes you past them and into the middle of Barnstable Harbor, on course for a return to your launch site. A good landmark on the mainland is a red-and-white communication tower, which sits just to the right of the inner-harbor entrance. The water is shallow out here, and if the wind is against you there may be some chop.

About 0.25 mile from the entrance to the inner harbor, you cross an east–west channel carrying boats to other landings on the mainland, including Salten Point, right. Soon you see the red and green poles marking the narrow channel from Barnstable Harbor to the inner harbor. With that channel immediately on your left, follow it into the entrance to the inner harbor. Your launch site is directly across the channel, left. Wait until the channel is clear to cross it. Or you may enjoy touring the inner harbor. If so, continue straight, passing boats moored in their slips, until you reach a dead end. Now paddle back along the opposite shore, passing the moorage for the whale-watching tour boat, until you reach the boat ramp and your launch site, both on the right.

TRIP 2   COTUIT, WEST, AND NORTH BAYS

Length: 8 miles

Highlights:

This scenic and adventurous tour around Osterville Grand Island takes you through four waterways: Cotuit, West, and North bays, and the Seapuit River, a narrow passage between the island and Dead Neck, a barrier beach fronting Nantucket Sound. One of at least two Dead Necks on the Cape, this one is home in summer to nesting terns and piping plovers. Its western tip, called Sampsons Island, is home to an active gull colony. The superb mansions of Osterville Grand Island, a secluded wooded upland, are lavish architectural creations best viewed from the water.

Nearby attractions

The Osterville Historical Society Museum on W. Bay Rd. in Osterville features a sea captain's home with art, antiques, a doll collection, and gardens; (508) 428-5861.

Tips

Launch about two hours before high tide for Nantucket Sound. Bring binoculars for birding.

Directions

From Rt. 6 eastbound in Sandwich, take Exit 2, signed for Rt. 130, Sandwich, and Mashpee. Follow Rt. 130 south 9.1 miles to Rt. 28. Turn left, go 0.1 mile to Main St. and turn right. Go 1.7 miles to Oyster Place Rd. and turn left. After 0.1 mile Oyster Place Rd. dead-ends at the Cotuit marina.

From Rt. 6 westbound in Barnstable, take Exit 5, signed for Rt. 149, Marstons Mills, and W. Barnstable. Go south on Rt. 149 toward Marstons Mills and Osterville. At 1.4 miles you come to a roundabout: proceed halfway around and continue south. At 3.8 miles you bear right, reach a stop sign, and then merge with Rt. 28. Follow Rt. 28 southwest 2.1 miles to Main St. and turn left. Go 1.7 miles to Oyster Place Rd. and turn left. After 0.1 mile Oyster Place Rd. dead-ends at the Cotuit marina.

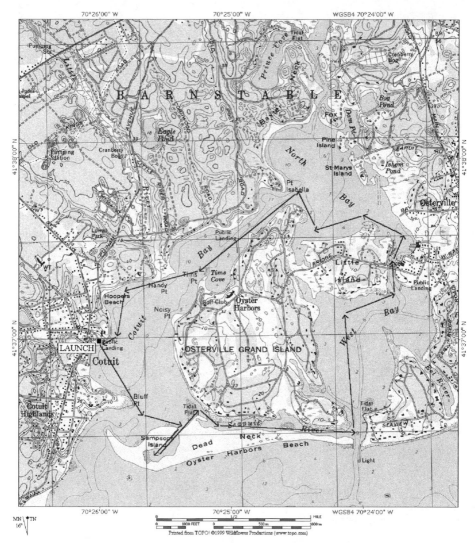

Trip 2—Cotuit, West, and North Bays

Parking and facilities

Most of the parking at the marina is resident-only from Memorial Day through Labor Day. But there are six first-come, first-served spaces along the north side of Oyster Place Rd. about 100 yards from the marina. These usually are full on summer weekends by Friday night. There are toilets at the end of Oyster Place Rd.

Launch

From either of two small sandy beaches that flank the wooden dock at the end of Oyster Place Rd.

Trip Description

As you paddle south away from the wooden dock and through the small but busy moorage you have one of the loveliest Cape scenes—the village of Cotuit—on your right. The church steeple and weathered buildings form a perfect backdrop for the boats at rest in the harbor. Many of the sailboats here are catboats, beamy crafts with a single sail and the mast set well forward in the bow. Be alert for the launch that shuttles people from the marina to their boats, and also for some of the birds that frequent this area, including greater yellowlegs and green heron. Across Cotuit Bay to your left is Osterville Grand Island, a mansion-studded wonderland that is the Cape's answer to Newport.

Keeping the main channel with its red and green markers well off to your left, a heading of about 170 degrees takes you past Bluff Point, a spit of land jutting east into Cotuit Bay. No-trespassing signs along the beach, right, warn you off, but you will be able to land on Dead Neck, ahead. Cotuit Bay, once famous for its oysters, opens to Nantucket Sound via a curvy passage that soon appears on your right. When no boats are approaching, cross the channel and make for Sampsons Island, which is the western end of Dead Neck.

Tug moored off Cotuit in Cotuit Bay

Sampsons Island is a bird refuge, and the screams and cries of gulls as you approach tell you it is an active rookery. In summer you will find the Cape's four common species—great black-backed, herring, ring-billed, and laughing—well represented here.

A salt pond in the middle of Sampsons Island is at the heart of the rookery, but from the direction you are coming its northeast-facing entrance is hidden. To find it, look for a break in the scrub vegetation that covers the island and then a sandbar stretching east. Just at the end of the sandbar, you turn sharply right and paddle through a shallow inlet and then into the deeper water of the salt pond. Gulls are everywhere, strutting on shore, sitting on nests, roosting in pine trees, and circling in the sky. Immature gulls have a habit of moving their heads up and down while tilting their bodies, similar to the teetering of certain sandpipers. Some experts say this enables the bird to get a better visual fix on a would-be predator through a crude form of triangulation.

Gulls, in addition to being notorious scavengers, are themselves supreme predators, and have devised curious methods for dealing with their generally hard-shelled or spiny prey. It is a common sight on the Cape to see a gull repeatedly pick up a clam and drop it from a great height onto a hard surface, such as a road or parking lot, until the clam's shell is smashed to bits. If fresh crab is on the menu, a gull will pull its scuttling dinner out of the water, flip the crab on its back, and use its bill to stab repeatedly at the crab's underbelly. I have even seen a great black-backed gull pull a very reluctant horseshoe crab out of the water by its tail, and some researchers have linked the worrisome decline in the horseshoe-crab population to predation by this species of gull.

Once you have paddled through the salt pond, return to its entrance and bear right on a heading of about 100 degrees, which soon brings you to the west end of the Seapuit River. Here a bulge of Dead Neck extends north and ends in a tidal flat, and as you move left into deeper water you have the boat channel immediately left, and then the bulk of Osterville Grand Island rising across the river. Keep a sharp eye out for boat traffic as you enter the river and stay alongside Dead Neck with the channel on your left. You may hear the sharp cry of a northern flicker echoing from the island's woodlands or the more insistent notes of a least tern overhead.

Osterville Grand Island, left, is heavily wooded with pines and oaks. Beautiful homes sit just back from the river on a low bluff, and most have large docks with powerboats moored alongside. In contrast, Dead Neck is a sparsely wooded barrier beach, with low dunes and scrub vegetation, beautiful in its own way. Just as you get past the tidal flat and into the river, there is a cove on your right where you can land and study the vegetation more closely. Poison ivy, salt-spray rose, seaside goldenrod, bayberry, pitch pine, eastern red cedar, scrub oak, and white oak all may be found here.

The Seapuit River is only about 100 yards wide here, and a heading of about 120 degrees keeps you just north of Dead Neck. Soon you pass a large salt marsh and tidal creek pushing north into Osterville Grand Island. On your right the low dunes and beach grass conceal protected nesting areas for terns and piping plovers, administered by Massachusetts Audubon Society. Piping plovers are listed as threatened under federal law, and least terns are on the Massachusetts list of special concern. Both species have been impacted by loss of nesting habitat, by increased disturbance during nesting season from people, pets, and off-road vehicles, and by predation.

At the east end of the Seapuit River you reach an inlet, right, linking Nantucket Sound with West Bay. If the seas are calm, adventurous kayakers can paddle out through this inlet, which is guarded by a breakwater, and explore Oyster Harbors Beach on the south side of Dead Neck. Otherwise, turn left at the east end of the Seapuit River, watching for boat traffic as you cross its channel, and make for a rock jetty protruding from Osterville Grand Island. Ahead is West Bay, a more-or-less circular body of water interrupted by a large finger of land jutting northwest into it. Your scenic route, now almost due north, stays between the main channel, right, and Osterville Grand Island, left.

Passing first the rock jetty and then a finger of salt marsh probing left, you paddle in shallow water, staying a few hundred yards offshore. Splendid homes decorate the shoreline, left. As you near the north end of West Bay you begin to turn right, staying parallel to the main channel. On your left is Little Island, an low-lying appendage of Osterville Grand Island, and another salt marsh. A heading of about 70 degrees allows you just to skirt a point of land on the southeast edge of Little Island. Once around it, you turn left and enter the narrow passage between West and North bays. Now you are in the main channel, approaching a drawbridge that carries car traffic from the mainland to Little and Osterville Grand islands.

Once past the bridge, you paddle through a large marina with a fantastic collection of powerboats and sailboats. Osterville, along with a handful of other Cape towns, was a boat-building center from the 1830s on. The village of Osterville is on your right, and North Bay is just ahead. North Bay is a popular water-ski area, so use caution if you go exploring there. If you want to land and stretch your legs, there is a town landing at the end of Bay St., across the main channel to your right. Otherwise continue through the marina and then curve left around the north side of Little Island. Your heading here is almost due west, and you paddle by a lovely salt marsh and a tidal creek, both left. As you near the northern tip of Osterville Grand Island, you pass an inlet, left, at the end of which are a picturesque windmill and also an osprey-nesting platform.

Now you turn north to skirt the tip of Osterville Grand Island, where more lavish homes sit back from the water's edge, and two wooden docks jut out into North Bay. Rounding the tip of the island, you turn left on a heading of about 310 degrees to enter a narrow passage between Point Isabella, right, and the island's tip. Staying just left of the main channel in the waterway connecting North and Cotuit bays, you come to a heading of about 260 degrees and pass a spit of land ending in a sandbar, left, forcing you away from shore. Once past it, you have Tims Point, a much larger spit, ahead, and also Tims Cove. Above the cove is Oyster Harbors, a luxury development complete with a golf course and a private beach. You may see a large schooner at anchor off Tims Point. She is the *Larinda*, a modified replica of a 1767 Boston schooner, a British sailing ship. Built over 26 years in Marstons Mills by Lawrence Mahan, her captain, the colorful 76-foot *Larinda* sports two masts and batten-lug sails. Launched here in 1996, she is available for private charters and special events. The *Larinda* winters in Falmouth, where she is open for tours.

Once past Tims Point, you bear across the bay for Handy Point, crossing the main channel. Even near high tide, the water off Handy Point is extremely shallow, so you stay well offshore. Some of the homes on the mainland,

Larinda, *replica of 1767 Boston Schooner, moored in Cotuit Bay*

right, feature steeply pitched roofs, quite different from those found on tradi-tional Cape salt-box cottages. And on Osterville Grand Island, left, huge man-sions, each with its own stairway to the shore, sit on a terrace that fronts steeply on the water. Passing Hoopers Beach, right, where you may find a sailboat race for kids in progress, you continue to skirt the shoreline until you reach the marina at Cotuit and your launch site.

Chapter 2

Bourne

TRIP 3　BASSETTS ISLAND

Length: 6 miles

Highlights

This enjoyable circuit of Bassetts Island, using Red Brook and Pocasset harbors, Buzzards Bay, and Hospital Cove, is a fine sample of what Cape Cod's west shoreline has to offer. Most of the journey is through protected waters, but the leg west of Bassetts Island is open to Buzzards Bay. Along the way you will see picturesque settlements around Hen Cove and Barlows Landing, as well as the less developed shoreline of Wings Neck and Scraggy Neck. Bassetts Island itself is part forested upland, part barrier beach, with only a few homes.

Nearby attractions

The Cape Cod Canal, which took five years to build, opened in 1914 and provided vessels plying the waters between Boston and New York with a safe alternative to the treacherous passage around the Cape. There is a 6.5-mile service road maintained by the US Army Corps of Engineers on the canal's south side that is perfect for hiking and biking. Access is from Freezer Rd., Sandwich; Pleasant St., Sagamore; and the southeast side of the Bourne Bridge. Kayaking in the canal is prohibited. Call the canal's recorded recreation hotline, (508) 759-5991.

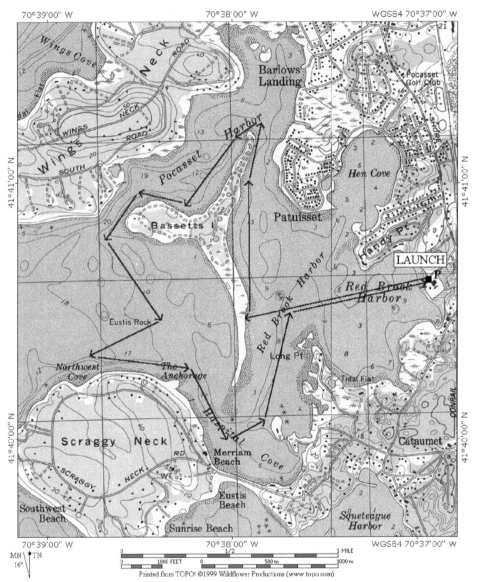

Trip 3—Bassetts Island

Tips

Launch an hour or two before high tide for Buzzards Bay. Land on the south finger of Bassetts Island at the beginning of the tour to check conditions west of the island. A strong current is possible in the narrows between Bassetts Island and Wings Neck at the southwest end of Pocasset Harbor.

Directions

From Rt. 6 northbound in Bourne, take Exit 1, signed for Rt. 6A and Sagamore. After exiting you are eastbound on Rt. 6A. Go 0.4 mile to Ben Abbey Rd. and turn left. Go 0.2 mile to a traffic signal at Sandwich Rd. and turn left. At 3.7 miles you bear left at a fork, signed for Rt. 6 West, and at 3.8 miles you come to a rotary. Go two-thirds of the way around and exit onto Rt. 28 South, signed for Falmouth and The Islands. Follow Rt. 28 south for 3.3 miles to Barlows Landing Rd., signed for Pocasset and Wings Neck, and turn right. At 1.7 miles you come to a stop sign at Shore Rd. and turn left (caution: this is not a four-way stop). Go 1 mile to the entrance to Kingman Marine, signed MARINE CENTER, which is just past Chauncy Way, a private road on your right. Turn right and go 0.2 mile to the parking area.

From Rt. 6 southbound in Bourne, after crossing the Sagamore Bridge, take Exit 1, signed for Rt. 6A and Sagamore. When you reach the traffic signal at Sandwich Rd. turn left, go 3 miles to the rotary, and follow the directions above.

Parking and facilities

Free parking is just one of the amenities in this wonderful complex. There are also rest rooms, telephones, a restaurant, a small store, and The Paddler's Shop, where you can buy or rent kayaks, sign up for tours, and talk with the helpful staff.

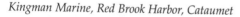

Kingman Marine, Red Brook Harbor, Cataumet

Launch

After parking, carry your boat to a small beach on the southwest edge of the parking area to the right of the lighthouse.

Trip Description

The west edge of Cape Cod, where it fronts Buzzards Bay, is a paddler's delight, with numerous coves, islands, beaches, and harbors to play in. Unfortunately, most of the parking in Bourne is resident-only during the summer, which is why Kingman Marine, in the village of Cataumet, is such a great spot. Its location on Red Brook Harbor gives you access to the protected waters of Hen Cove, Pocasset Harbor, and Hospital Cove, and to Bassetts Island, a three-fingered landmass wedged between the outstretched arms of Wings Neck to the north and Scraggy Neck to the south. Beyond their sheltering confines lie the open waters of Buzzards Bay, awaiting ambitious and adventurous kayakers.

Buzzards Bay, like so many other features on the Cape, was a product of the great ice sheet that covered this area during the last ice age. One arm of this ice sheet, called the Buzzards Bay Glacier, left behind a moraine that created the Elizabeth Islands and the west shore of Cape Cod. This moraine continues from Falmouth north and then northeast to Sandwich, where it joins another that runs west–east. From early times, Buzzards Bay was an important waterway, and shortly after the Pilgrims settled in Plymouth they established a trading route to it from Cape Cod Bay, using Scusset Creek, the Manomet River, also called the Monument River, and a short overland section, that avoided the long and dangerous sea journey around the Cape's outer arm. For large craft, however, the outer route was the only option, and shoals off the Cape's Atlantic shore became a graveyard for ships and men. The Cape Cod Canal, opened in 1914, changed all that, making it possible for deep-water vessels to pass safely between Buzzards Bay and Cape Cod Bay.

As you paddle away from the beach on a heading of about 260 degrees, you pass through one of the largest boat moorages on the Cape, full of powerboats and sailboats, some quite magnificent. With markers for the main channel on your left, you make for Long Point, a spit of land jutting north into Red Brook Harbor. The low sandy form of Bassetts Island is dead ahead, and behind it rises the forested bulk of Scraggy Neck, almost an island but connected to the mainland by a narrow strand. Now passing Long Point, left, you paddle over to Bassetts Island, watching for boat traffic as you cross the north–south channel, and land on the sandy beach about 0.25 mile from its south tip. After landing, an easy walk over low dunes stabilized by beach grass and poison ivy gives you a view west of the open water leading out to Buzzards Bay. If conditions are favorable you can make a complete circuit of

Bassetts Island. If they are not, you can continue north to Barlows Landing and Pocasset Harbor, then return via Hen Cove and Handy Point.

To circle the island, paddle north along its east shore, with Handy Point across Red Brook Harbor to your right. Just left of Handy Point is the entrance to Hen Cove, an oval body of water in the village of Pocasset. As you work your way toward the north tip of Bassetts Island on a heading of about 10 degrees the waterway narrows. The island's shoreline curves away to the left and then back to the right, but you can stay parallel to the main channel, which is to your right. The island is higher and more wooded here, and posted with NO TRESPASSING signs. After you pass green can 11, right, you paddle through the narrows separating Red Brook and Pocasset harbors. If you want to go ashore, there is a fine beach at Barlows Landing about 0.5 mile northeast. The gray-shingled facades of houses fronting a small marsh, right, and pleasure-craft moored just outside the channel complete this picturesque scene.

As you round the north tip of Bassetts Island, you have ahead Wings Neck, a long arm of land pointing southwest into Buzzards Bay. The lighthouse at its tip was erected in 1848, cast its beacon brightly for about 100 years, and now is privately owned. Just back from the beach, left, are salt-spray roses and stands of eastern red cedar, along with pines and oaks. Staying a few hundred feet off the rocky shoreline, you paddle southwest, with the main

Barlows Landing, Pocasset Harbor

channel to your right. Soon the shape of the island forces you to turn west, and you pass an osprey-nesting platform, left. More rocks, in the form of large boulders, keep you well offshore here. In the narrows between Bassetts Island and Wings Neck there is the potential for a strong current, especially on an outgoing tide. This may combine with wind and seas from Buzzards Bay to create difficult conditions, so take time here to examine things carefully before proceeding.

Once through the narrows, you have submerged rocks jutting out from the west tip of Bassetts Island on your left. Continue paddling southwest toward a red can until you are well clear of the rocks. (If conditions are favorable, you can paddle west along the shore of Wings Neck to view the lighthouse up close.) Now you turn left and on a heading of about 160 degrees come in line with the middle of Bassett Island, about 0.25 mile to your left. Continue paddling on a southward course until you draw near Scraggy Neck. You can now turn right and explore its shoreline to Northwest Cove and beyond, or turn left to pass through The Anchorage and enter Hospital Cove.

The homes on Scraggy Neck are set on a bluff, with riprap and seawalls protecting them from the tidal surges that accompany big storms. Even on a calm day, you may begin to feel swells sweeping in from Buzzards Bay when you reach Northwest Cove. Once you have finished exploring, head east to The Anchorage, a boat moorage, and then turn southeast toward Hospital Cove, the body of water just ahead. As you do so, keep well offshore to avoid rocks, but try to stay out of the main channel, left. As you pass red can 2, left, you can move closer to the shore on your right, where more boats may be moored. A heading of about 170 degrees here will take you into Hospital Cove, another boat moorage.

Ahead is Merriam Beach and a low, sandy strand, topped by a road, that connects Scraggy Neck with the mainland. A south wind blowing unimpeded here can roil Hospital Cove and even produce small waves, but these will help you on your journey back to Red Brook Harbor. As you come into the cove, you begin to make a left turn, keeping the main channel on your left. A heading of about 30 degrees will let you paddle safely between offshore rocks on your right—look for a marker with the word SHOAL—and red can 8 on your left. Keep the same heading until you pass Long Point, right, and red can 10, left. Once clear of the point you can begin to turn right and, watching for boat traffic, paddle back through the boat moorage to your launch site, just left of the lighthouse, on a heading of about 90 degrees.

Chapter 3

Brewster

TRIP 4   CLIFF AND LITTLE CLIFF PONDS

Length: 3 miles

Highlights

This tour, which includes a short portage, takes you around Little Cliff and Cliff ponds, in the heart of Nickerson State Park. Little Cliff, one of the clearest ponds on the Cape, is ringed with a variety of trees and shrubs that attract birds, making it ideal for birding. Cliff, one of the deepest of the Cape's many glacier-formed kettle ponds, is surrounded by steep hillsides holding a lovely mix of pines and oaks.

Nearby attractions

These ponds are within Nickerson State Park, which also has camping, canoe and kayak rentals, and trails for hiking, biking, and horseback riding; (508) 896-3491.

Tips

Nickerson State Park is open for day use from dawn to dusk. Go early in the morning, and try to avoid summer weekends. Bring binoculars or practice "birding by ear" around Little Cliff Pond.

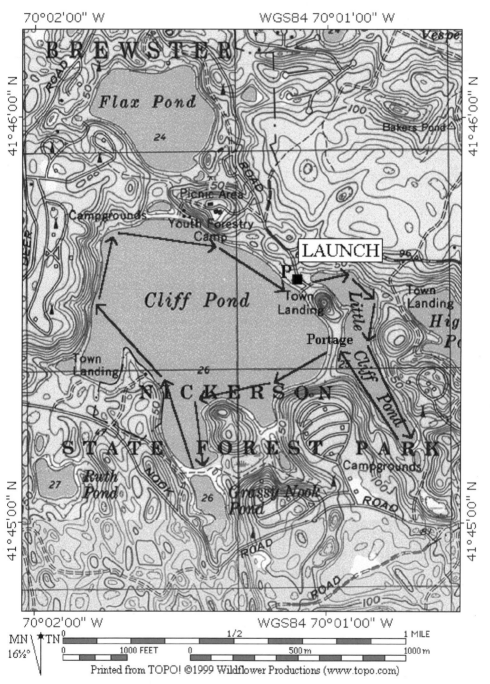

Trip 4—Cliff and Little Cliff Ponds

Directions

From Rt. 6 northbound in Orleans, take Exit 12, signed for Rt. 6A, Orleans, and E. Brewster. At Rt. 6A turn left and go 1.5 miles to the Nickerson State Park entrance, left. Stop at the entrance kiosk to pick up a map showing ponds, hiking trails, bike paths, equestrian trails, campgrounds, and picnic areas. Continue past the entrance kiosk, now on Flax Pond Rd. At 0.3 mile Flax Pond Rd. turns left and Deer Park Rd. continues straight. You turn left and go another 1.1 miles to the parking area for Cliff and Little Cliff ponds. Just past the parking area, the road continues several hundred feet to a boat ramp on Little Cliff Pond, left, and a beach on Cliff Pond, right.

From Rt. 6 southbound in Orleans, take Exit 12, signed for Rt. 6A, Orleans, and E. Brewster. At Rt. 6A turn right, go 1.4 miles to the Nickerson State Park entrance, left, and follow directions above.

Parking and facilities

Day use and parking are free. There are toilets in the parking area.

Launch

From the boat ramp on Little Cliff Pond.

Little Cliff Pond, Nickerson State Park

Trip Description

The land for Nickerson State Park was donated in 1934 to the state by the widow of railroad executive Roland G. Nickerson to honor her husband and also their son, who died in World War I. The drive from the entrance kiosk to the parking area for Cliff and Little Cliff ponds is one of the prettiest on the Cape, taking you through a forest of pines planted in the 1930s by the Civilian Conservation Corps. When you reach the ponds, take a moment to get acquainted with some of the Cape's typical flora, including pitch pine, white oak, black oak, bayberry, sweet pepperbush, and of course poison ivy. The small trees with curious mitten-shaped leaves are sassafras, whose roots and root bark are used to make tea, provide scent for soap, and flavor root beer. Around the edge of Little Cliff Pond grow military rushes, pickerelweed, and white water lilies.

After launching, drift quietly close to shore for a moment. The tall trees surrounding this narrow pond may be alive with bird song. Listen for the "enk, enk, enk" call of the white-breasted nuthatch, the "potato chip, potato chip" flight note of the American goldfinch, or the falling-then-rising "pee-a-wee" song of the eastern wood-pewee. Sometimes you can identify a bird by watching its behavior. Eastern kingbirds, in the flycatcher family, sit upright on a perch, dart out to catch insects, and then return to the same perch. Gray catbirds, in the same family as mockingbirds and thrashers, tend to stay well-hidden in dense cover.

This is one of the clearest ponds on the Cape, and as you paddle clockwise around it, you may see schools of small trout as well as an occasional bass. When you come upon a cluster of water lilies, you can see how they are anchored by long stalks to rhizomes, or roots, buried in the mucky bottom. Although this is a small pond, there are many indentations in the shoreline to explore, and as you head south into deeper water you pass a stand of common reeds (*Phragmites australis*), an invasive plant that some ecologists view as a pest. At the south end of the pond is a sandy beach that makes a lovely spot to land, to spread out a picnic, or to go for a swim. South of the beach is a much smaller pond, rich in frogs, toads, snakes, and turtles. Many of the Cape's deeper ponds have such adjoining wetlands, which may be water-filled only in spring.

Continuing your circuit of Little Cliff, perhaps serenaded by a chorus of frogs, you reach the west side of the pond, where a low sandy barrier separates it from its larger neighbor to the west. Mixed in with the white water lilies here are bullhead lilies sporting large yellow flowers. Ahead is another stand of common reeds. Before you reach it, turn left and land in a little cove. From here you can portage to Cliff Pond, which is just a few hundred feet away over a low rise. The beach here on Cliff Pond is used by the Brewster

Day Camp, and you may see groups of young people swimming, sailing, or paddling canoes and kayaks. About 0.25 mile to the northwest is the beach at the end of Flax Pond Rd.

Launching into Cliff Pond, you bear left and begin a clockwise circuit by heading west. Once you leave the beach area the shoreline narrows and becomes rocky, evidence of the glacial moraine that formed this part of the Cape. Back from the water's edge is a dense forest, mostly pitch pines, clinging to the hillside. Ducks and Canada geese love this pond, and in summer you can see them herding their young in the shallows near shore. Passing a

Cliff Pond, Nickerson State Park

small cove, left, you round a high, steep-sided promontory and then enter a larger cove at the south end of Cliff Pond. If you want to land, the sandy beach here makes a fine spot. After landing, walk south about 100 yards across a low sandy divide to visit Grassy Nook Pond, which may be drying up and turning into a bog. Its remarkable collection of water lilies was stranded on the mud when I arrived during the summer-long drought of 1999. Once you have enjoyed this secluded spot, paddle north out of the cove and then bear left around the next promontory, keeping a sharp eye and ear out for powerboats, which unfortunately are allowed on this otherwise small and quiet pond. The powerboats launch into the cove, left, from a town landing just off Nook Rd. Cross the mouth of the cove carefully and continue heading northwest to the pond's west shore.

On shore the almost-pure stands of pine are slowly but relentlessly giving way to a mixed forest of pine and oak, as is the case on most of the Cape. This process, called forest succession, often hastened by logging, has taken place several times since the Cape was settled. A narrow, sandy beach fronts this side of the pond, where soon you paddle past a collection of massive boulders, called glacial erratics, left behind when the vast ice sheet that once covered this area retreated. Beyond the boulders is a wider stretch of beach

Brewster Day Camp offers boating opportunities on Cliff Pond

fronting the state park's Area 4 campground. Now at the north end of the pond you turn right, passing a low-lying area that marks the divide between Cliff and Flax ponds. The shoreline left looks inviting, but it is posted with many warning signs and belongs to the Youth Forestry Camp. As you turn southeast and approach the beach at the end of Flax Pond Rd., watch for swimmers. Before you reach the roped-off swimming area, turn left and land. You are just about 150 feet from your launch site on Little Cliff.

TRIP 5   WALKERS POND AND UPPER MILLPOND

Length: 4 miles

Highlights

This easy trip takes you through Walkers Pond and Upper Millpond, two lovely and largely undeveloped bodies of freshwater where non-motorized travel predominates. The ponds are surrounded by dense forest interspersed with marshlands, and this makes for good birding, especially early in the morning, when the air is cool and the insects plentiful. Bald eagles have been seen here, and the nearby woodlands provide daytime roosts for black-crowned night-herons.

Nearby attractions

The Cape Cod Museum of Natural History is just west of Paines Creek Rd. on Rt. 6A in W. Brewster; (508) 896-3867. The Punkhorn Parklands, 800 acres of conservation lands with trails for birding, hiking, and bicycling, are located just southeast of Walkers Pond and Upper Millpond. For maps and information call the Brewster Conservation Commission, (508) 895-3701, ext. 135.

Tips

Bring binoculars for birding.

Directions

From Rt. 6 in Harwich, take Exit 10, signed for Rt. 124, Harwich, and Brewster. Follow Rt. 124 south 0.2 mile to a flashing yellow light at Queen

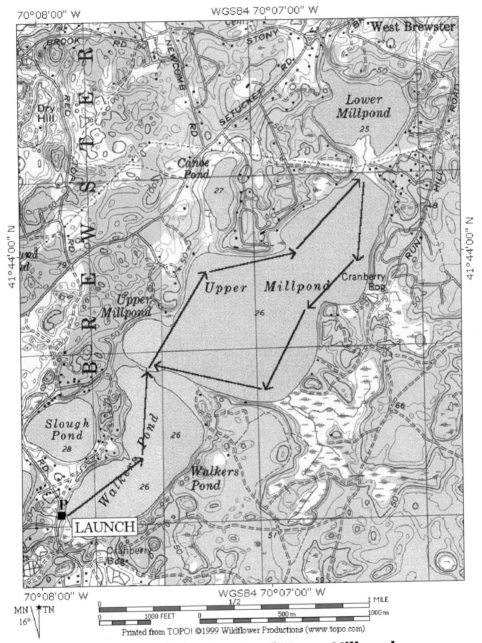

Trip 5—Walkers Pond and Upper Millpond

Cut between Walkers Pond, Upper Millpond

Anne Rd. Turn right and go 2.5 miles to Main St. in N. Harwich. Bear right onto Main St. and go 0.3 mile to Depot St. (Depot St. is not signed, but across Depot St. is Main St. Extension, signed NOT A THROUGH ROAD.) Turn right onto Depot St., which becomes Slough Rd. as you enter Brewster. Go a total of 2 miles from Main St. to a paved parking area on the right.

Parking and facilities

From Memorial Day through Labor Day, 9 A.M. to 3 P.M. parking is by a permit, which can be bought at the Brewster visitor center, located in the basement of town hall, 2198 Main St. Call the visitor center (508) 896-3800 or the permit office (508) 896-4511. There are daily, weekly, biweekly, and seasonal permits available for residents and non-residents alike.

Launch

There is a boat ramp for Walkers Pond, and a narrow muddy beach next to it, several hundred feet northeast of the parking area. Access is via a paved road on the parking area's east side.

Trip Description

Walkers Pond, Upper Millpond, and Lower Millpond, referred to locally as the Brewster Ponds, are favorite kayak and canoe spots. Lower Millpond, on the northeast end of this three-link chain, catches water from the other two, and this explains its name. Water from the ponds was used to drive America's first water-powered grist mill, built in 1663 north of Lower Millpond. Today, a mill built in 1873 stands on the same location just off Stony Brook Rd. Visitors to the mill in spring may see runs of alewives moving up Stony Brook from Cape Cod Bay into the ponds. Bordering the ponds to the southeast are the Punkhorn Parklands, 800 acres of forest, meadows, and freshwater marshes enjoyed by birders, hikers, and bicyclists.

Walkers Pond, a mostly undeveloped wilderness, is ringed with vegetation right to its waterline. Here you will find many of the Cape's common trees and shrubs, including pitch pine, red maple, black oak, white oak, swamp azalea, and sweet pepperbush. The vine-like water plant bordering parts of the pond is water willow. It has arching branches up to 9 feet long holding whorls of lance-shaped leaves and, in summer, pink flowers. Leaving the launch site, you paddle close to the pond's west shore, listening to the wind rustling the maple leaves and perhaps spying a great blue heron cruising over the pond.

Because this pond is undeveloped, chances are you will see few if any other people even in summer, so take your time and savor this rare solitude. Rounding a rocky point, you pass a secluded house, left, and then head

White water lily is common on the Cape's ponds

northeast toward the low barrier of land between Walkers Pond and Upper Millpond. There are several cuts through the barrier, and depending on the water level you may be able to paddle through. If not, you can easily drag your boat through one of the cuts. Look for a sandy spot amid the greenery, about a quarter of the way from where the barrier joins the west shore of Walkers Pond. That marks one cut, and about 200 feet to its left is another, but it is rocky and overgrown.

As you approach the barrier, you may notice a small shorebird that takes flight with stiff wing beats and teeters up and down after it lands. This is a spotted sandpiper, one of the few shorebirds found along the shores of fresh-water ponds and in salt marshes. Spotted sandpipers breed throughout most of the US and Canada, and winter in Central and South America. Near shore, you may notice pickerelweed, erect water plants with heart-shaped leaves and spikes of blue-violet flowers. On the pond's sandy bottom you may see pond mussels, mollusks whose curious life-cycle includes several weeks spent as tiny parasites on fish. The most common species of pond mussel is called the alewife floater. On the sandy barrier between Walkers Pond and Upper Millpond you will also find wild grape, wild rose, Virginia creeper, and poison ivy.

Once in Upper Millpond, you begin a clockwise circuit along its scalloped northwest shoreline. Just after you launch you may see a collection of lily pads floating on the water to your left. The ones with white flowers are called white water lilies, and the ones with yellow flowers are bullhead lilies, also called yellow pond lilies. Each lily pad has a long stalk that reaches down to a rhizome, or root, buried beneath the pond's sandy bottom. This pond is more developed than Walkers, with homes set back from the water's edge and a few sailboats moored here and there. Look here for a green heron, the great blue's diminutive cousin, skulking along the shoreline or flying to and from roosts in the tall trees that ring the pond.

Nearing the pond's north end, you paddle by several wooden docks, left, and a few rock boulders on the shore, deposited when the last ice-age glaciers departed. The Cape's kettle ponds, as they are called, are among the area's most scenic and best-loved features. They range in depth from a few feet to more than 80 feet, and in extent from dozens to hundreds of acres. Overhead a set of powerlines traverses the narrow passage between Upper Millpond and Lower Millpond. Here a sandy-bottomed creek, whose banks are choked with vegetation, carries water north about 250 yards from one pond to the next. It is possible to drag your boat through this passage, but you have to be willing to do some serious bushwhacking. (Restoration in the fall of 1999 stabilized the shoreline around the passage to insure continued access to Upper Millpond for migrating alewives.)

Instead, turn south and then southwest to continue your circuit of Upper Millpond, passing more glacial boulders and a rocky outcrop jutting west from the shoreline. There are several coves on this side of the pond to explore, fronted by steep, wooded hillsides, and you soon have the Punkhorn Parklands—forested uplands alternating with low-lying marshy areas—on your left. Now the barrier between Upper Millpond and Walkers Pond forces you to begin turning right, and you soon reach one of the cuts you used earlier. From here portage or paddle through to Walkers Pond and then continue a clockwise exploration of its shoreline or simply retrace your route to the launch site.

Chapter 4

Chatham

TRIP 6   FISH PIER TO CROWS POND

Length: 3.6 miles

Highlights

This shuttle trip, which can be done as a round-trip if you don't have a shuttle or want a longer paddle, takes you from the Fish Pier in Chatham Harbor past Tern Island, through Bassing Harbor and the south end of Pleasant Bay, and into Crows Pond. Some of the Cape's most scenic water-front vistas are along this route, and for much of the paddle you are in protected water only a few hundred feet offshore.

Nearby attractions

The Fish Pier has an observation deck from which you can watch the fishing boats unloading their catch, usually in mid-afternoon.

Tips

Launch around high tide for Chatham Light, which is about 1.5 hours earlier than high tide for Pleasant Bay. If the wind is from the north, reverse the trip's direction and paddle from Crows Pond to the Fish Pier and launch at high tide for Pleasant Bay. Passage around the east side of Tern Island, an alternate route, can be tricky—attempt it only during calm conditions and at slack high tide.

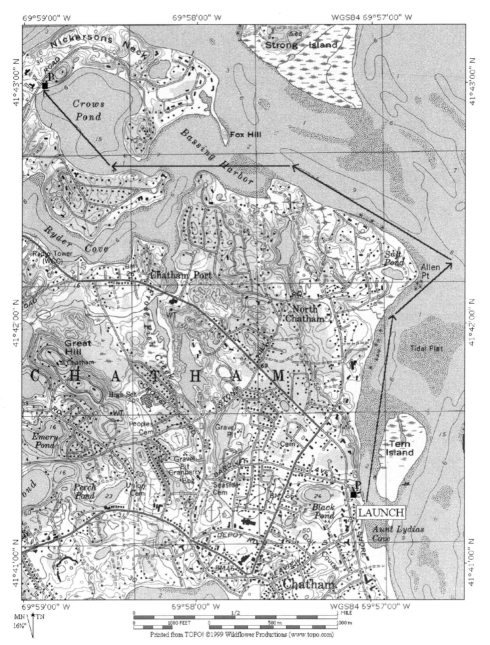

Trip 6—Fish Pier to Crows Pond

Directions

This is a shuttle trip, starting at the **Fish Pier** and ending at Crows Pond. Drive first to **Crows Pond**, leave a car there, and proceed to the Fish Pier.

To reach **Crows Pond**: From the Rt. 6 rotary at the Eastham-Orleans line, follow Rt. 6A/28 south 0.5 mile to a fork where Rt. 28, signed for Chatham and Falmouth, branches left. Bear left, go 6.3 miles to Fox Hill Rd., and turn left. Go 0.6 mile to a town landing, right, just across the road from the Eastward Ho Country Club.

From the rotary in Chatham, follow Rt. 28 (signed here as Rt. 28 South) northeast and then northwest 3 miles to Fox Hill Rd. Turn right and go 0.6 mile to a town landing, right, just across the road from the Eastward Ho Country Club.

To reach the **Fish Pier**: Follow Fox Hill Rd. back to Rt. 28 and turn left. After 2.2 miles, you reach a junction with Shore Rd. Here Rt. 28 turns right, but you continue straight 0.3 mile to the Fish Pier, left, and park in the upper parking area.

Parking and facilities

At Crows Pond there are a small parking area, a boat ramp, and a sandy beach. At the Fish Pier there are a large parking area, a harbormaster's office, rest rooms, and Nickerson's seafood market.

Town landing at Crows Pond, early morning

Launch

From the sandy beach just south of the Fish Pier.

Trip Description

Settled by Pilgrims in 1656 and incorporated in 1712, Chatham soon joined
Harwich and Barnstable as one of the Cape's foremost fishing ports. From
here Chatham's fishermen sailed forth to the Grand Banks, the Nantucket
Shoals, and the icy waters off Nova Scotia in search of cod. It undoubtedly
would have amazed them to hear that the Cape's namesake fish may today
be in danger of disappearing due to over-fishing. Today, Chatham Harbor,
including the waters around the Fish Pier, is one of the busiest harbors on
Cape Cod, so use caution as you launch, especially during mid-afternoon
when the fishing boats are coming in to unload their catch. On your right is
Aunt Lydias Cove, and to your left, separated from the mainland by a narrow
waterway, is Tern Island, home in summer to hundreds of nesting terns and
shorebirds. Across the harbor is Nauset Beach, a long ribbon of barrier beach
that is part of Cape Cod National Seashore.

This barrier once ran unbroken along the east side of Pleasant Bay and
Chatham Harbor to near the north tip of Monomoy Island, giving protection
from the Atlantic Ocean. But a January 1987 northeaster radically altered the
landscape by creating a break in Nauset Beach at a point almost directly
across from Chatham Light, a little more than a mile south of the Fish Pier.
The Chatham Break and its adjacent waters are now considered among the
trickiest and most potentially dangerous on the Cape because of currents and
heavy surf. The formerly unbroken barrier is now divided into two parts,

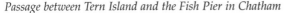

Passage between Tern Island and the Fish Pier in Chatham

Nauset Beach and South Beach. Nauset Beach runs south unbroken from Orleans to the Chatham Break, where its south end is referred to as North Beach. South Beach, which over the years has attached itself to the mainland south of Chatham Light, extends south and comes to an end east of Monomoy Island. Just to make things more confusing, Monomoy itself is really two islands—North Monomoy and South Monomoy. Nauset Beach and South Beach are enjoyed by swimmers, picnickers, fishermen, birders, and marine-mammal enthusiasts.

Now you turn north on a heading of about 20 degrees and paddle through a narrow boat moorage between Tern Island and the mainland. One of the reasons to do this trip around high tide is to avoid the swift southward current that flows here when water from Pleasant Bay empties into the ocean through Chatham Harbor. This is a picturesque area, with fishing boats tethered to colorful floats, and the low sandy expanse of Tern Island alive with birds. The island is a bird refuge administered by Massachusetts Audubon Society, and if you land here you must observe all restrictions and stay out of nesting areas. There is a small marsh on the island's north end, well-guarded by shallows and sandbars. As you pass Tern Island, you have the beautiful waterfront homes of North Chatham to your left and the entrance to Pleasant Bay ahead. Stay well offshore to avoid hidden rocks, and aim for a small cove just southwest of Allen Point, also called Minister's Point. There is a narrow tidal creek leading through a salt marsh on the south side of the cove that you can explore if the tide is high enough. Regardless of the tide, the beach that fronts this cove makes a good landing spot if you need to get out of your boat. From here you have a fine view south toward Tern Island and the Fish Pier.

Now turning northeast on a heading of about 70 degrees, you skirt the sandbar and shallows that extend east from Allen Point. Once around the point, you swing northwest on a heading of about 310 degrees and paddle just offshore, passing more beautiful homes, wooden piers, moored boats, and several public beaches. If it is windy—and this area often is—boats moored on a single bow line will swing too and fro, so be alert as you thread your way through them. Also keep a sharp eye for working shellfish boats. Markers to your right show the main channel, and you can easily avoid it. Farther right is Strong Island, a triangular landmass that sits in the south end of Pleasant Bay, just east of Nickersons Neck. (The north side of Strong Island is a fine spot for landing, picnicking, and hiking.) As you enter Bassing Harbor on a heading of about 290 degrees watch for boats entering or leaving Ryder Cove, a good place to explore when it isn't too busy.

Passing the entrance to Ryder Cove, left, you have on your right Fox Hill, a low-lying hump connected to the mainland at low tide. Directly ahead is the entrance to Crows Pond, a circular body of saltwater bordered on the north by Nickersons Neck. Once in the pond, you turn right to a heading of about 320 degrees and paddle among the many boats that find safe moorage here. Many fine homes are tucked away in the woods that ring this scenic body of water. When you reach the pond's northwest shore, land on the sandy beach just right of the boat ramp.

TRIP 7  **OYSTER POND TO LITTLE MILL POND**

Length: 7 miles, plus an 0.6-mile walk

Highlights

This loop, one of the most enjoyable on the Cape, takes you through Oyster Pond, the Oyster Pond River, Stage Harbor, the Mitchell River, Mill Pond, and Little Mill Pond. A town best viewed from the water, Chatham has a little of everything, including fine New England homes, bustling harbors with watercraft of every shape and size, secluded salt marshes, sandy beaches, and forested uplands. A pleasant stroll along Main St. completes the loop and takes you back to the launch site.

Nearby attractions

Monomoy Island National Wildlife Refuge and adjacent South Beach are two of the northeast's best birding spots. Access is by boat, and tours are offered by the Wellfleet Bay Wildlife Sanctuary, (508) 349-2615, and by the Cape Cod Museum of Natural History, (508) 896-3867.

Tips

This trip is best done around the time of high tide for Stage Harbor. Because you have a short walk to retrieve your car, bring on board walking shoes or sandals and a small pack to carry valuables you do not want to leave in your boat. You may also wish to have a cable and lock if you are going to leave your boat unattended for more than a few minutes.

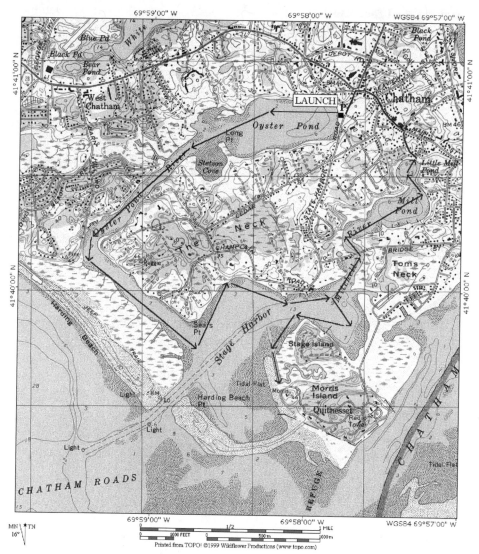

Trip 7— Oyster Pond to Little Mill Pond

Directions

From the Rt. 28 rotary in Chatham, follow Stage Harbor Rd. southwest 0.1 mile to the parking area, right, for Oyster Pond. Use the second entrance, near the rest rooms, for easier beach access.

To retrieve your boat, return on Stage Harbor Rd. to the rotary, turn right onto Main St., and go 0.4 mile to Mill Pond Rd. Turn right and go 0.1 mile to a town landing at the north end of Little Mill Pond.

Parking and facilities

There is a large public parking area here with rest rooms that unfortunately may be locked.

Launch

From the sandy beach just right of the roped swimming area.

Trip Description

After leaving the swimming area, which may be crowded in summer, you paddle west along the north shore of Oyster Pond, a oval-shaped body of water connected to Stage Harbor by the Oyster Pond River. Because this is a relatively safe passage out to Chatham Roads and Nantucket Sound, you will pass many boats moored in the pond and along the river's banks. Fine homes are tucked away in the forested hills that ring the pond. Chatham is one of the Cape's loveliest towns, and one of the best ways to enjoy it is from the water. Staying a couple of hundred feet offshore, you continue west on a heading of about 280 degrees. Soon you bear left to pass a small point of land jutting south into Oyster Pond, and then paddle by a cove ringed with salt marsh on your right. Stay between a shellfishing area, right, and the well-marked main channel, left. Long Point and Stetson Cove are across the channel to your left.

Sail boat plies the waters of a tidal creek between Morris and Stage Islands

Entering the Oyster Pond River, you have a marina, the Chatham Yacht Basin, ahead and a narrow inlet on your right.

Continue paddling straight through the boat moorage, passing a pier and a steep boat ramp, right. The riverbank is lined with docks and many berths for powerboats. Beautiful wood-shingled homes perch on the bluff above the river, right, and steep stairways lead from them down to the docks. If the tide has turned, you may begin to feel a current aiding your downstream efforts. You may also begin to notice a breeze blowing in from Nantucket Sound, which is to the southwest. Once through the boat moorage the river bends slightly left, and soon you pass another marina, the Oyster River Boat Yard, on your right. Now the river makes a 90-degree bend to the left, and its character changes dramatically. A large salt marsh opens up on your right, and beyond it are the low dunes that mark Hardings Beach (shown on the USGS map as Harding Beach), which fronts Nantucket Sound. The old Stage Harbor Light, decommissioned in 1935 and now privately owned, sits on a bluff overlooking Hardings Beach and the break in it that forms the entrance to Stage Harbor. The keeper's house is in the traditional four-cornered design, with a steeply pointed gable on each side.

The salt marsh behind Hardings Beach has many delightful tidal channels that run through it, and if the tide is high you can explore these and view some of the shorebirds that call them home during spring, summer, and fall. Among the most common are willets, greater yellowlegs, and least sandpipers. Willets are large sandpipers, drab gray for most of the year but speckled with brown during spring and summer breeding season. In flight, or when they raise their wings, a striking black-and-white pattern can be seen. Greater yellowlegs are slightly smaller sandpipers with yellow legs, mottled gray and brown bodies, and a long, dark bill. They can easily be identified by their rapid "tu-tu-tu" calls, usually given in flight. Both of these sandpipers are regularly seen wading in shallow water. Least sandpipers are tiny shorebirds with light-colored legs and a black bill, found on mudflats and in drier reaches of salt marshes.

Continuing down the Oyster Pond River, you turn southeast on a heading of about 160 degrees, paddling or perhaps just drifting with the current toward Stage Harbor. The harbor, named for fish-drying racks, or stages, is formed by the protective arms of Hardings Beach and a hooked spit of land extending east and then northeast from Morris Island. The main channel from Nantucket Sound goes through the middle of Stage Harbor on a northeast–southwest line just ahead. The entrance to Stage Harbor from the Oyster Pond River is marked by Sears Point—when the old lighthouse is at 3 o'clock, Sears Point will be the right-angled corner of land on your left. Turning left to round it, watch for boat traffic running between Stage Harbor and the Oyster Pond River. Now on a heading of about 70 degrees, you stay several hundred feet from the shoreline, left, along a body of land called The Neck. The high ground across Stage Harbor to the right is made up of Morris Island and, to its north, Stage Island. Both are connected to the mainland by a low causeway, so they are not true islands. A meandering tidal creek, which you can explore later, flows partway between them. About 0.3 mile northeast of Sears Point is a small town landing with a sandy beach, and this makes a fine spot to get out of your boat and stretch your legs.

Underway again, you paddle close to shore, heading southeast, and soon reach the narrows north of Stage Island. A long wooden pier juts out from the left and the main channel is immediately right. Wind and tidal currents can make for a tricky passage here, and you need to keep a sharp eye and a keen ear out for boat traffic. Looking right, you can see the expanse of Stage Harbor and the break leading out to Chatham Roads and Nantucket Sound. A yacht basin and more piers are on your left, and soon, perhaps aided by wind and following seas, you are propelled into a protected cove at the mouth of the Mitchell River. This is a popular boat moorage and there is a town landing at the end of Stage Harbor Rd., left.

Touring the cove clockwise, you paddle by the mouth of the Mitchell River, left, and then, passing an inlet, also left, turn south toward the Morris Island causeway. Just northeast of the causeway, bordered by salt marsh, is Outermost Harbor, a departure point for organized tours to Monomoy Island and South Beach. As you round the north tip of Stage Island, you are back in the open water of Stage Harbor, and if the wind is against you the paddling may be tough. Soon, however, you reach the shelter of the creek that partly separates Stage and Morris islands. Turning left you enter its peaceful confines, and on the right there is a bit of beach where you can land. Canada geese are fond of this area, and you may also see a white-winged scoter, a black sea-going duck with a yellow bill, white eye patches, and white wing bars.

If the seas are calm, you can return to Stage Harbor, turn left, and paddle out to Hardings Beach Point, the spit of land connected to Morris Island. If not, retrace your route to the north tip of Stage Island, then cut across the cove on a heading of about 70 degrees toward the mouth of the Mitchell River. Ahead is a set of red and green channel markers that you keep on your left. When you pass red can 12 you swing left to a heading of about 40 degrees and paddle toward the bridge over the Mitchell River. Stage Harbor Marine, a boat yard, is left, and the salt marsh on your right is favored by snowy egrets. Watching for boat traffic, you paddle under the bridge and pass a town landing, left.

About 100 yards past the bridge the river makes a sharp bend to the right, and your heading is now about 80 degrees. The river here is broad and there is a finger of land pointing toward you from the shoreline, right. Passing this, you enter Mill Pond, where you may see people standing in boats using long metal rakes to scrape the pond's bottom for hard-shell clams, a procedure called bull raking. This pond is ringed with gorgeous homes, many two or three stories, sided with gray weathered shingles, and finished with white trim and green shutters. Ahead is a town landing and the Godfrey Windmill, built in 1797. The mill, used to grind corn, needs winds of at least 20 mph to turn its massive stones.

Turning left here, you paddle through a narrow passage that leads north to Little Mill Pond. When you reach the town landing at the pond's north end, land on a narrow strip of beach just left of a wood pier, watching carefully for boat anchors that may be lying hidden in shallow water. If you want to lock your boat, there is a convenient signpost—the sign reads LIMIT OF TOWN LANDING—just up from the water's edge. Stow all your gear in the boat's cockpit and cover with your spray skirt. Be sure to remove all valuables and don't forget your car keys! Now you are ready for a delightful walking tour of Chatham on the way to retrieve your car.

The street heading north from the town landing is Homestead Lane, and the street curving left is Mill Pond Rd.. Turning onto Mill Pond Rd., you walk uphill 0.1 mile to Main St. where you turn left. Chatham is known for its

Picturesque tug completes the scene on Mill Pond

restaurants, clothing shops, book stores, and picturesque churches, so this is a fine place to dawdle if you have the time. At its junction with Seaview St., Main St. veers left, and soon you reach the Rt. 28 rotary, with the First Congregational Church on your right. Here Stage Harbor Rd. goes left, but to stay on the sidewalk you must first cross the road and then turn left. In about 0.1 mile you reach the parking area for Oyster Pond.

Chapter 5

Dennis

TRIP 8   SESUIT HARBOR TO QUIVETT CREEK

Length: 8.5 miles

Highlights

This out-and-back route takes you out of Sesuit Harbor into Cape Cod Bay and then along the shore of Quivett Neck to Quivett Creek, whose waters flow through a large salt marsh wedged between the bay and Rt. 6A. The opportunity to paddle in Cape Cod Bay plus the chance to view bird and plant life up close in a large and beautiful salt marsh make this a rewarding trip.

Nearby attractions

Scargo Lake, just off Rt. 6A a few miles west of School St., features two freshwater beaches and a stone observation tower with great views. The tower is reached via Old Scargo Hill Rd. off Rt. 6A. The Cape Cod Museum of Natural History, a wonderful place to learn about the area's flora and fauna, is 1.7 miles east of School St. on Rt. 6A; (508) 896-3867.

Tips

Launch an hour before high tide for Cape Cod Bay. The stretch from Sesuit Harbor to Quivett Creek is in open water and exposed to northerly winds.

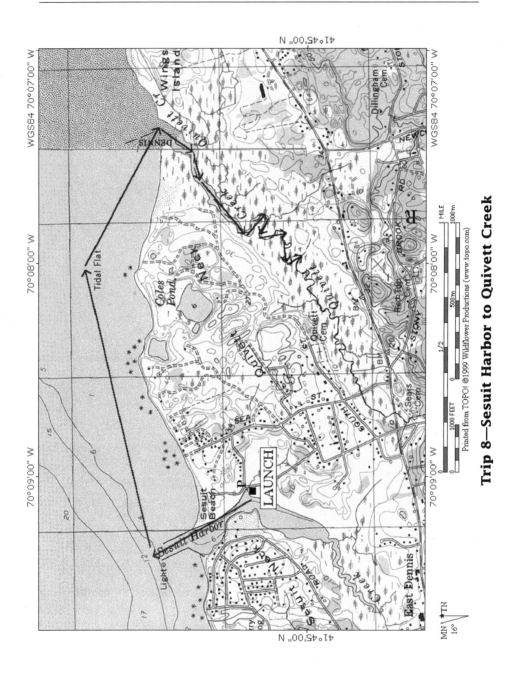

Trip 8—Sesuit Harbor to Quivett Creek

Directions

From Rt. 6 in Dennis take Exit 9, signed for Rt. 134, Dennis, and W. Harwich. Follow Rt. 134 north 3.2 miles to a traffic signal at Rt. 6A. Turn right, go 0.8 mile to School St. and turn left. Go 0.3 mile to Pleasant St., turn right and then immediately left onto Cold Storage Rd. Go 0.3 mile to the Sesuit East Marina parking area, left.

Parking and facilities

The parking area and boat ramp are operated by the Massachusetts Public Access Board. During summer there is a small fee for parking and boat launching. Use is free during the rest of the year. There are toilets at the south end of the parking area.

Launch

From the boat ramp at the northwest corner of the parking area.

Trip Description

Like the towns of Bourne and Brewster, Dennis was named for its pastor, Rev. Josiah Dennis, whose 1736 manse, or home, stands off Whig St. east of Rt. 6A. In early days the town—which split off from Yarmouth, its neighbor to the west—had a small fishing fleet, most of which took to Nantucket Sound from a harbor on the Bass River. A few, however, plied the waters of Cape Cod Bay and wintered in Bass Hole and Quivett Creek, your destination. As you leave the boat ramp, you are in the mouth of Sesuit Creek, which drains Scargo Lake and leads to Cape Cod Bay, right. In the 19th century, Sesuit Creek was the location of the Cape's most famous shipyards, run by the sons of boatbuilder Asa Shiverick—Asa Jr., Paul, and David. In the 1850s

Kayakers in Cape Cod pass Quivett Neck

and early 1860s they launched eight full-rigged clipper ships and barks into the bay. Across from you is the Northside Marina, a large boat moorage with a café and an ice-cream stand. Stay to the right and watch for boat traffic in this busy area. The mouth of the creek here is a deep channel with two rock jetties extending out into the bay. As you near the end of the jetties, you may begin to feel the swells sweeping in from the open water to the north. Now past the jetties and in Cape Cod Bay, you turn right and paddle parallel to the shore on a heading of about 90 degrees. The lovely white-sand beach here, crowded in summer, appears on local maps as Cold Storage Beach but on the USGS map as Sesuit Beach.

The low dunes behind the beach are covered with beach grass, and behind them on a bluff is an assortment of homes, some of them impressively large. Even around high tide the water is shallow here and there are near-shore boulders, deposited by the retreating glaciers, to avoid. As you paddle by the first of two blunt points of land, stay well offshore—this area, a tidal flat, is left high and dry twice each day, and you can come back in six hours to walk or pedal, rather than paddle, this part of the route. In summer you may notice small gulls with a black bill, dark eyes, a gray mantle, and black-tipped wings floating on the water. These are young laughing gulls, similar in appearance to adults of the species but lacking their black hood.

Reflections in still waters of Quivett Creek

With the great expanse of Cape Cod Bay on your left, you continue paddling east and soon pass the second of two points, this one fronted by a number of on-shore rocks. The outer reaches of Quivett Neck, consisting of sandy shoreline and low dunes, are now on your right. This area, traversed by only a few rough dirt roads, is mostly undeveloped, but families in four-wheel-drive vehicles manage to find their way to the beach for swimming and picnicking. Turning right on a heading of about 140 degrees, you aim for the mouth of Quivett Creek, an inlet between Quivett Neck and Wings Island to the east. This is a twisting tidal creek which flows generally southwest through a vast salt marsh and forms part of the town line between Dennis and Brewster, its neighbor to the east.

The entrance to the creek is guarded by a wedge of salt marsh. Once around it, you paddle into the creek's wide mouth, where boats may be moored and people may be swimming. This is a fine place to land and get out of your boat, either now or on your return journey. Now entering the creek proper, you paddle on a lazy ribbon of water bordered variously by salt marsh and a forest of pitch pines, black oak, and eastern red cedar. If you arrive here at high tide, you will feel a slight current pushing you upstream as the tidal flow continues to work its way into the marsh. Just upstream from its mouth, the creek forges a deep channel and the water is crystal clear, refreshed by the twice-daily cycle of the tides. Farther up, the water becomes brackish, sluggish, and chocolate brown.

Although it is little more than a mile as the crow flies from the creek's mouth to the end of navigable water near Sea St., the paddling distance is more because of the creek's many slalom-like twists and turns. A few homes are set back in the trees on the south side of the marsh, left, and you can only envy their location. As you proceed farther into the marsh, you may notice that the marsh grasses are getting taller. The dominant plant of low-lying salt marshes, saltwater cordgrass, gives way in more brackish conditions to its cousin freshwater cordgrass, a tall plant that in summer bears large, bristly spikes of tan-colored flowers. Common in the marsh are great blue herons, and you may see their lanky, prehistoric-looking forms lift gracefully into the air as you approach.

Soon you come upon an osprey-nesting platform to the left of the creek. Many such platforms have been erected in Cape marshes, and the raptors they are designed to attract, once in peril because of DDT, have staged a remarkable comeback. In early summer you may see a pair of ospreys busily shuttling back and forth from the bay bringing meals of fresh fish to their youngsters. Ospreys are classed among the hawks, kites, and eagles, and are now commonly seen on the Cape and elsewhere along the Atlantic coast. Just past the nesting platform, if you look to your right, you can see Quivett

Cemetery, located at the end of South St. Quivett Creek, so clear near its mouth, is here a rusty brown. Another common marsh plant, marsh elder, can be found along its banks. It has somewhat leathery, serrated leaves that vary from egg- to lance-shaped, and greenish white flowers held aloft on spikes.

Although you can paddle farther up the creek, the channel becomes narrow and overgrown. The vicinity of the osprey-nesting platform makes a good turn-around spot, and if you time your visit right you can drift back down the creek on an outgoing tide. There is a lag of about an hour between the turn of the tide at the creek's mouth and when the current reverses this far upstream. For your return to Sesuit Harbor, leave the creek mouth on a heading of about 320 degrees, and when you are several hundred yards offshore, bear left to about 270 degrees, lining up with the jetties in the distance. In summer an afternoon breeze usually kicks up from the southwest, and this may push you offshore, so you may need to correct your course. As you approach the harbor entrance, watch carefully for boat traffic.

Chapter 6

Eastham

TRIP 9  **GREAT POND**

Length: 1.8 miles

Highlights

This easy trip makes a fine first-time paddle or one to share with children. The pond is ringed with a large variety of native plants and also affords good opportunities for birding, especially in the secluded cove at the pond's southwest corner.

Nearby attractions

First Encounter Beach, so named for an altercation with local Native Americans that took place during the third and last discovery voyage by a small party from the *Mayflower*, is on Cape Cod Bay at the end of Samoset Rd.

Tips

In summer arrive early in the day to avoid the crowds.

Directions

From Rt. 6 in Eastham, follow Samoset Rd., signed for First Encounter Beach, west 0.5 mile to Great Pond Rd. Turn right and go 0.1 mile to a beach and town landing, left.

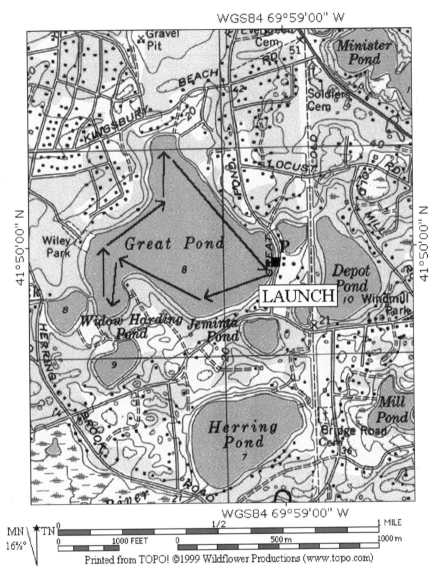

Trip 9—Great Pond

Parking and facilities

Parking is along the left (west) side of the road. In summer there is a small parking fee for non-residents. There is a seasonal toilet at the north end of the parking area.

Launch

From the boat ramp at the south end of the parking area or from the sandy beach just to its north.

Trip Description

This is the largest of six Great Ponds on the Cape, the others being in Bourne, Falmouth, Provincetown, Truro and Wellfleet. At 109 acres it could easily encompass both of its rivals, but its maximum depth, 36 feet, is 20 feet shallower than that of Wellfleet's Great Pond, and only a foot deeper than Truro's. All three, like most on the Cape, are kettle ponds, formed by the melting of great chunks of buried ice left behind by the retreating glaciers at the end of the last ice age. Kettle ponds depend on rainwater and groundwater to replenish water lost through evaporation and hence are quite susceptible to pollution. Human activities that once were not given a second thought, such as bathing with soap and shampoo, and watering dogs and horses, are now generally frowned upon and even prohibited in certain ponds.

The beach here on the pond's east shore is very popular and crowded during summer, and the swimming area is marked by ropes and floats. After a careful launch, you begin a clockwise tour of the pond by paddling southwest, passing clumps of pickerelweed growing in the water close to shore. This freshwater plant, common in the Cape's ponds, grows erect with heart-shaped leaves and spikes of violet-blue flowers. Set back from the water's edge is a mixed forest of pines and deciduous trees, lake-front homes peeking out through the foliage. A few boats—small sailboats and motorboats—are moored just offshore in shallow water. Because it is close to Cape Cod Bay, this pond attracts some of the birds normally seen near saltwater, including gulls and terns. Gulls generally float on the water, whereas terns are usually seen sweeping though the air, hovering, and then diving for fish.

Each of the Cape's towns has its own distinctive character and special attractions, but Eastham is often overlooked by people on their way to enjoy Wellfleet's art galleries or Provincetown's night life. Yet some of the Cape's most beautiful scenery—Nauset Marsh, Fort Hill, the Red Maple Swamp—is right here, along with places of historical interest, including a windmill built in 1680 in Plymouth and brought to Eastham in the 1800s, and First Encounter Beach, where the newly arrived Pilgrims and the Native Americans exchanged arrows and musket fire. Eastham is also home to one of the two Cape Cod National Seashore visitor centers, located just off Rt. 6 about a mile northeast on Salt Pond.

If you stay close to shore, you will be able to investigate some of the Cape's common freshwater and woodland plants. In addition to pickerelweed, water willow is at home along the margins of our ponds and is found here. Water willow is a vine-like plant with arching branches up to 9 feet long, pointed leaves arranged in whorls, and, in summer, pink flowers. Growing on shore nearby are sweet pepperbush, wild grape, wild rose, poison ivy, and sweet gale, a bayberry relative.

As you round a point of land jutting northwest and enter a small cove on the pond's southwest corner, you pass a stand of tall pitch pines, magnificent trees. The Cape's pines, so intimately linked with its character, are in many places slowly giving way to oaks and other deciduous trees, in a process called forest succession. The Cape has been logged several times to provide timber for ships and houses, and when Thoreau visited in the mid-19th century he found the area from Barnstable to Orleans "for the most part, bare, or with only a little scrubby wood left on the hills" and the outer Cape "an

Summer means boating for fun on Great Pond

apparently boundless plain." Yet just 50 years before, a traveler on the Cape had commented on the "lofty" forests of Truro, and many of the towns obtained all the wood they needed locally and even exported surplus to Boston. Henry C. Kittredge, in his classic history of the Cape, says this "wanton" over-harvesting, so out of keeping with the otherwise frugal nature of the Pilgrims and their descendants, led to the demise of farming on the Cape and, of necessity, the rise of seafaring: "...it drove the Cape Cod farmer to the sea for a livelihood; and there he won such fame as no farmer can ever hope for."

According to *Birding Cape Cod*, Great Pond is "one of the best freshwater ponds for birding on the Outer Cape." Among its regular fall, winter, and spring visitors are pied-billed grebes, mute swans, ring-necked ducks, scaup, hooded mergansers, and ruddy ducks. You may be surprised to see a large wading bird fly out from the trees. This is a black-crowed night-heron, and as its name implies, it hunts and feeds at night in nearby salt marshes. During the day it roosts in trees, commonly with other herons. Some herons and egrets do just the opposite, hunting by day and roosting at night. Among these are the green heron and the snowy egret, two other common Cape birds. Using the trees here not as a roost but as a hunting perch may be an eastern kingbird, a member of the flycatcher family. This small gray-and-white bird darts out from its perch to snag insects on the wing.

Now paddling north out of the small cove, you pass an overgrown passage, left, choked with poison ivy, that leads to Bridge Pond. Just ahead, a public beach adjacent to Wiley Park has a roped-off swimming area, which you keep well on your left. The area around Wiley Park and Bridge Pond is dominated by Atlantic white cedar, a tree found in swamps. In Massachusetts, Atlantic white-cedar swamps are considered to be threatened plant communities. Heading north, you enter another small cove, this one at the pond's north end. The trees leaning over the water here are red maple, a species that is aggressively spreading throughout the northeast to the detriment of less adaptable hardwood varieties. Other trees and shrubs here include black oak, northern arrowwood, blueberry, and swamp azalea. Lovely homes fronted by beautifully manicured lawns adorn this part of the shoreline. As you turn southeast in shallow water to return to the launch site, you may notice the shells of pond mussels, a freshwater variety of mollusk, scattered on the pond floor. As you approach the beach watch for swimmers and for other boats launching from or returning to the ramp.

TRIP 10  NAUSET MARSH

Length: 5 miles

Highlights

One of the best paddling trips on Cape Cod, this semi-loop tour of scenic Nauset Marsh in Cape Cod National Seashore starts at Salt Pond and visits Salt Pond Bay, Nauset Bay, and the tidal creeks that flow through the north half of this vast salt marsh. The birding is superb, especially during spring and fall migrations, when thousands of shorebirds visit the marsh to rest and feed.

Nearby attractions

Cape Cod National Seashore's Salt Pond visitor center is east of Rt. 6 immediately north of Salt Pond; (508) 255-3421. Fort Hill, the Penniman House, and the Red Maple Swamp are reached via Gov. Prence and Fort Hill roads, east of Rt. 6 a little more than 1 mile south of Salt Pond.

Tips

Timing is critical for this route: launch at high tide for Nauset Beach, Orleans. The tide for the marsh lags several hours behind, so you will have high water where and when you need it most. (If you want to explore the marsh at mid-tide, Creek A is a good option.)

Directions

From Rt. 6 in Eastham, 0.2 mile south of Cape Cod National Seashore's Salt Pond visitor center, turn east onto Salt Pond Landing Rd. and go several hundred feet to a parking area and a town landing on Salt Pond.

Parking and facilities

Parking is free but limited to about 6 cars. There is a seasonal toilet here. The nearby visitor center has a large parking lot, rest rooms, water, phone, books, maps, interpretive displays, and helpful staff.

Launch

From the town landing just north of the parking area.

Trip 10—Nauset Marsh

Trip Description

Nauset Marsh is a vast and complex system of salt-marsh islands and tidal creeks bordered on the west by hilly woodland adjacent to Rt. 6 and on the east by a long strand of low dunes and barrier beach that extends south, with one break, to Chatham. Eroded by the Atlantic's stormy fury during winter months, and augmented by current-deposited sand during quieter times, the beach, and especially the break where it is open to the ocean, is constantly shifting, and the marsh's waterways change depth from year to year. The entire strand from Eastham to Chatham is called Nauset Beach on the USGS map, and along it are individual beaches with their own names. The beach east of Nauset Marsh is commonly called Coast Guard Beach, and most locals reserve the name Nauset Beach for the stretch of Atlantic coastline from Orleans to Chatham.

Nauset Marsh was explored and charted in 1605 by Samuel de Champlain, who noted Native American settlements along its shores. In 1620 the Pilgrims sailed by Coast Guard Beach on their way to their landing site in Provincetown. Thoreau walked by the marsh during his visits to Cape Cod in the 1840s and 50s. Henry Beston's dune cottage, memorialized in his 1928 classic, *The Outermost House*, stood on the sand spit at the south end of Coast Guard Beach until a furious storm in 1978 swept it away. Nauset Marsh and its environs are the subject of another wonderful book, *The House on Nauset Marsh*, published in 1955 by Wyman Richardson, a Boston physician and Harvard Medical School professor. Clearly this swath of mud and marsh has the power to entrance and enchant!

After launching you paddle southeast on a heading of about 120 degrees across Salt Pond, a glacial kettle pond, to the inlet connecting it with Salt

Passage from Salt Pond to Nauset Marsh

Pond Bay and the wide expanse of Nauset Marsh. The marsh, mudflats, and dunes here are prized by birders, who come to witness the spring and fall shorebird migrations, the daily flights of herons and egrets, the mating and parenting antics of terns and piping plovers, the assembly of wintering ducks and geese, and such specialties as black skimmers and American oyster-catchers. When you reach the inlet, you paddle through it and soon enter Salt Pond Bay. Ahead the flooded marsh looks like a huge lake. Hemenway Landing, Skiff Hill, and Fort Hill are in the distance to your right. Most of the water in the marsh is shallow even at high tide, but as you turn left you can take advantage of a deep channel that hugs the shoreline.

On a heading of about 100 degrees, you work your way along the north side of Salt Pond Bay. In the middle of the marsh, slightly right of your bow, is an osprey-nesting platform, one of many in the Cape's salt marshes. On shore to your left you may see hikers and bicyclists using the trail from the Salt Pond visitor center to Coast Guard Beach. The trees along the shoreline here are mostly eastern red cedar, the most widely distributed conifer in the East. Actually a type of juniper, its wood is used for fence posts, chests, cabinets, and carvings. In fall, cedar waxwings congregate in flocks to feed on the cones, which resemble small berries and have a gin-like fragrance.

Leaving the channel as it turns into a small cove, left, you aim for a boat-house situated on a point of land just ahead. This point marks the northeast border of Salt Pond Bay, and just opposite it, to your right, is the first of three tidal creeks that cut through Nauset Marsh, and the one you will use on your return. I have labeled it Creek A on the map for this route. Just past this creek, a crooked finger of salt marsh juts northwest and the waterway you are in narrows to about 100 yards. Ahead in the distance are Nauset Bay and the old Coast Guard station that sits above Coast Guard Beach. After its career as a life-saving station ended, the building became the headquarters of the newly formed national seashore and now serves as a residential environmental-education facility.

Still parallel to the shoreline, you paddle northeast, now on a heading of about 70 degrees. The entrance to Nauset Bay is marked by a second point of land, which just lines up with the Coast Guard station as you approach. There may be a few boats hauled up on shore near the point or moored just off it. When you reach the point, the second creek through the marsh, marked in summer with colorful lobster buoys, is on your right. This is Creek B. The bay here is extremely shallow, even at high water, so you turn slightly right and change your heading to about 80 degrees. The east and southeast sides of Nauset Bay are some of the last places to flood as the tide rises, and during times of peak shorebird migrations—April/May and August/September— the remaining exposed mudflats here may be crowded with hundreds or

Salt Pond Bay, Nauset Marsh

thousands of birds. At high tide, you may find many birds roosting on the sandy flat between the marsh and the dunes behind Nauset Beach. During late spring and summer, the dunes here and elsewhere in places on the Cape are roped off and closed to the public to protect nesting terns and piping plovers, the latter listed as threatened under federal law. This is also a good place to look for American oystercatchers and black skimmers.

If you are visiting during the nesting season and you want to land, you may do so on the beach on the east side of Nauset Bay. Farther south on the spit, landing is difficult at high tide because most of the beach that remains above water is roped off. As you paddle across Nauset Bay on its south side you come upon several islands of salt marsh, barely exposed at high tide, that guard the entrance to the third creek, Creek C. The entrance to this creek faces almost due north and you turn sharply right to enter it. If you are here in summer, your passage may be disputed by one or more large shorebirds called willets. These are drab gray birds, except during breeding season when they take on a speckled brown appearance. In flight, however, they present a striking black-and-white wing pattern that immediately proclaims their identity. Their territorial behavior, indicative of nesting, includes flying straight at an intruder and veering off only at the last moment, and making raucous vocalizations.

Once you turn into Creek C, here a broad waterway, you are paddling almost due south with a large, sandy flat backed by dunes to your left, and salt marsh to your right. Soon a narrow creek merges from the right, and now you have the osprey-nesting platform off your bow at about 2 o'clock. Stay to the right here, because there is a shallow sandbar that stretches almost all the way across the creek ahead. If it is too shallow you may have to get out and drag your boat for several hundred feet. Once past the sandbar your creek widens and is joined on the right by Creek B.

As you come out of the narrow confines of the creek and into the open, the water gets much deeper and you may see an assortment of lobster buoys ahead. Beyond them is a small island of salt marsh. About 100 yards to your left is the back side of Coast Guard Beach, where at this point the last remaining clumps of dune grass give way to bare sand. Just about a mile farther south is the opening to the Atlantic Ocean. In years past you could paddle to it, but now this part of the marsh has silted in and is too shallow even at high tide. If it is not nesting season and the beach to your left is not roped off, you can land there. Otherwise, just before reaching the small island of salt marsh turn right, and stay right as you enter a broad waterway on a heading of about 320 degrees. The Coast Guard station is off in the distance at about 3

Common tern rests atop a lobster buoy

o'clock and the osprey-nesting platform is to its left. Just to the right of your bow is the boathouse opposite the entrance to Creek A.

Among the gulls commonly found here in summer are great black-backed, herring, and laughing gulls; and among the terns you may see are least and common terns. Also here are least sandpipers and, occasionally, spotted sandpipers, a mostly freshwater species. If you have time, and the inclination to do more birding, you may want to explore some of the tidal creeks leading into the marsh on your right. Many are dead ends and quickly get too narrow to turn your boat around, so you need to be adept at paddling in reverse. Across the water to your left is a narrow creek, dotted in summer with buoys, that leads to Hemenway Landing. Ahead the waterway forks, with Creek A on the right and a passage into the south end of Salt Pond Bay on the left. Now in Creek A, you move left to avoid a shallow area and paddle along its west side, heading north. With the boathouse in sight, cross to the northeast corner of Salt Pond Bay and from here retrace your route to the launch site.

Chapter 7

Falmouth

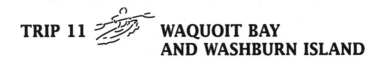

TRIP 11   **WAQUOIT BAY AND WASHBURN ISLAND**

Length: 7.5 miles

Highlights

Very few paddling trips on Cape Cod offer the scenic variety and pure enjoyment found on this circuit of Washburn Island, which uses the Childs and Seapit rivers, Waquoit Bay, Vineyard Sound, and Eel Pond. If Vineyard Sound is too rough, or you want a shorter trip, you can make an easy portage from a salt pond at the southwest corner of Washburn Island to Eel Pond. A longer or alternate excursion can be made by visiting Dead Neck and Sage Lot Pond at the south end of Waquoit Bay. Overnight camping in a pine forest on Washburn Island is available by reservation; (877) 422-6762.

Nearby attractions

Waquoit Bay National Estuarine Research Reserve (see **Directions** below) has an excellent visitor center with natural history displays, literature, and helpful staff. There are also hiking trails, interpretive programs, and a children's play area; (508) 457-0495.

Ashumet Holly and Wildlife Sanctuary, run by Massachusetts Audubon Society, has a self-guiding nature walk on trails that circle a coastal-plain kettle pond. Rare wildflowers, holly trees and other exotics, along with native plants, are the attractions of this wonderful 45-acre preserve located on Ashumet Rd. just north of Rt. 151. near the Falmouth/Mashpee line.

Tips

Launch a few hours before high tide for Falmouth. Carefully assess conditions in the Vineyard Sound before deciding whether to make a complete circuit of Washburn Island or to portage from the salt pond to Eel Pond.

Directions

From Rt. 6 in Sandwich, take Exit 2, signed for Rt. 130, Sandwich, and Mashpee. Follow Rt. 130 south 9.1 miles to Rt. 28 and turn right. At 2.3 miles you come to the Mashpee rotary, where you go half-way around and continue on Rt. 28 toward Falmouth. At 5.8 miles you pass the entrance, left, to the Waquoit Bay National Estuarine Research Reserve headquarters and visitor center. At 6 miles you cross the Childs River and then turn immediately left onto Whites Landing Rd., a paved road just past Edwards Boat Yard. Go about 100 yards to a town landing with a boat ramp, left, on the west bank of the Childs River.

Parking and facilities

Park in the lot on the corner of Rt. 28 and Whites Landing Rd., just west of Edwards Boat Yard. If you are camping on Washburn Island, overnight parking is allowed here. At the boat yard are toilets, telephone, cold drinks, and the Waquoit Kayak Company, an outfitter that offers rentals, sales and tours from the beginning of May through Columbus Day.

Launch

From the boat ramp or the muddy shore adjacent to it at the end of White's Landing Rd.

Trip Description

Launching and then turning right, you leave Edwards Boat Yard behind you and head downstream on the placid waters of the Childs River, whose source is a few miles north at Johns Pond in Mashpee. Piers with boats moored alongside line the river, and lovely homes sit back from its shores. Falmouth has a number of narrow waterways, most of them called ponds even though they are not completely enclosed, fronting Vineyard Sound. This creates a fjord-like shoreline with fingers of land jutting south from Rt. 28. The paddling opportunities here are superb, and this trip is just one of many possible ones. Falmouth's largest sheltered body of water is Waquoit Bay, just to the east of the Childs River and connected to it by a short waterway called

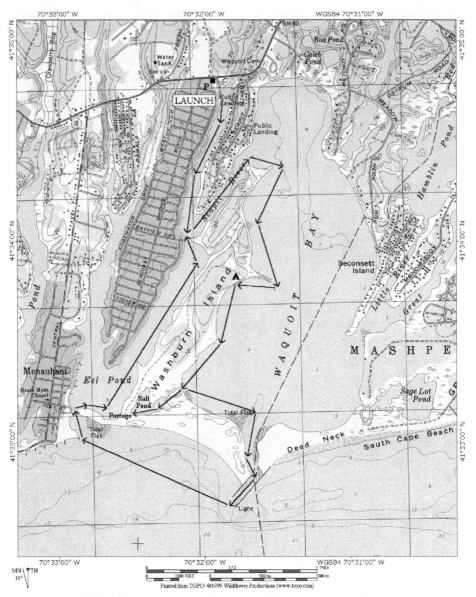

Trip 11—Waquoit Bay and Washburn Island

the Seapit River. On Waquoit Bay's west shore is L-shaped Washburn Island, where campsites are available for kayakers and other boaters.

Settled by Quakers from other Cape towns and their supporters in the late 17th century, Falmouth played a role in the Revolutionary War when its citizens, along with those from neighboring Sandwich, repulsed a fleet of British ships intent on burning the town, the only notable engagement of the war on Cape soil. The town rose to prominence as a whaling port in the mid-1800s and with the coming of rail service in the 1870s soon became a resort community for the well-to-do from Boston and New York. Today the town boasts 68 miles of coastline, 12 miles of beaches, a world-famous oceanographic institute in Woods Hole, a road race in August that attracts elite runners, and ferry service to Martha's Vineyard.

Soon you reach the junction of the Childs and Seapit rivers, and here you turn sharply left, now with the west side of Washburn Island on your right. The island is named for Albert H. Washburn, a Dartmouth professor and minister to Austria in the 1920s who had a family house here. This side of the island is closed to watercraft but there are many landing sites on the Waquoit Bay side. On your left are more homes, piers, and boats, and back from the shoreline stands a mixture of pines and oaks. Washburn Island, however, is undeveloped and has many pure stands of pitch pine. On a heading of about 55 degrees you paddle in clear but shallow water, with a channel flanked by red and green markers ahead. Staying to the right of the channel, you near the north tip of Washburn Island, where an osprey-nesting platform rises above the sandy shore. Spotted sandpipers and semipalmated plovers are among the shorebirds to look for here.

As you swing right around the island's tip and into Waquoit Bay you may have to move farther offshore to find deeper water. The north end of the bay

View south from a campsite on Washburn Island

is home to many sailboats and powerboats, but much of the rest of the bay, which resembles a large pond, is very shallow. On its south side, between Washburn Island and Dead Neck, is a narrow opening to Vineyard Sound. Now on a heading of about 210 degrees, you paddle in deeper water about 100 yards from the east shore of Washburn Island, right. This side of the island consists mostly of low dunes with scrub vegetation and a pine-and-oak forest dominated by pitch pines. In fact it is very reminiscent of the outer Cape, especially Wellfleet's Great Island, which is described elsewhere in this guide.

About one third of the way down the island's east shore, you paddle around a sand spit jutting into the bay and then turn right to enter a large cove. In the woods fronting this cove is the campsite area, and you may see boats hauled up on shore or anchored just off and tents pitched in the pines. The beach on the cove's north shore makes a good place to land, and from here, if you like, you can access the hiking trail that runs the length of Washburn Island. The island's 11 rustic campsites—9 for families up to five and two for groups up to 25—can be reserved by calling (877) 422-6762. The campsites are merely clearings in the forest, but some campers adorn them with elaborate tents, tarps, hammocks, and beach chairs. There is no drinking water and no open fires are allowed. There is a small per-night fee, and summer weekends fill many months in advance.

Leaving the cove and heading southwest, you pass a finger of salt marsh on the right and then use a heading of about 240 degrees to paddle along the shoreline and put you in line for the entrance to a tidal creek at the inside angle of Washburn Island's L. On shore, the pines are here joined by stands of eastern red cedar, actually a variety of juniper. The mouth of the tidal creek is right, and if the tide is high you can turn up it to visit a salt pond at the island's southwest corner. The creek immediately forks but the two branches soon rejoin. Take the left-hand fork, which is slightly deeper, and paddle until you reach the south edge of the salt pond, where there is a small beach on which to land. This is a good spot to examine some of the Cape's native marsh and seaside plants, including saltwater cordgrass, salt hay, glasswort, sea lavender, beach grass, salt-spray rose, bayberry, marsh elder, and of course poison ivy.

A short path leads from the beach across a low sandy strand to a vantage point overlooking beautiful Vineyard Sound. From here you can look southeast to Martha's Vineyard, a little more than 5 miles away. You can also assess conditions in the sound to decide if you want to continue the circuit of Washburn Island or to portage a few hundred yards west to Eel Pond. If you decide to portage, pick up the route description from Eel Pond below. If conditions in the sound are favorable, retrace your route out of the salt pond and

Salt pond, Washburn Island

the tidal creek to Waquoit Bay. Now you turn right, and on a heading of about 130 degrees paddle parallel to the shoreline, soon reaching the main channel, indicated by red and green markers, that links Waquoit Bay with Vineyard Sound. On an outgoing tide, a strong current runs through the narrow passage between Washburn Island and Dead Neck as the bay drains into the sound.

Here you have several options. You can head directly out into Vineyard Sound to continue your circuit of Washburn Island. Or you can first cross the channel and land on Dead Neck, get out of your boat and have a picnic or go for a hike on South Cape Beach, a state park. Or you can continue paddling east and explore Sage Lot Pond on the southeast corner of Waquoit Bay. To continue around Washburn Island, paddle into the narrow passage between the island and Dead Neck, staying clear of any boat traffic, and stay on its right-hand side. Two parallel rock jetties create an opening to the southwest, and once past them you are in Vineyard Sound. Now turning right to a heading of 310 degrees, you have the south shore of Washburn Island on your right and Martha's Vineyard in the distance on your left. Ahead about 1 mile is your goal, the entrance to Eel Pond.

Even on calm days in summer, Nantucket Sound, the water behind you that here joins Vineyard Sound, usually has long swells running from the south which may push you toward shore. Try to hold your course by sight-ing on riprap on the shoreline just west of the inlet to Eel Pond. Near the inlet are rocks, some just above the surface at high tide, projecting south from Washburn Island that you must avoid. With a red channel marker in sight, you paddle almost to the riprap before turning right into the inlet to Eel Pond. A deep channel hugs the west side of the inlet. Watch for boat traffic here as you paddle past the Menauhant Yacht Club, left. Stay left to avoid the shallows projecting west from a small sandy island, right, that was once the very west tip of Washburn Island. Just past the yacht club, with red can 8 ahead, wait until it is safe to cross the channel by turning right.

This part of Eel Pond is a beautiful boat moorage, extremely scenic, with many fine sailboats. On a heading of about 110 degrees you paddle toward Washburn Island, passing the cut that created the sandy island at the inlet's mouth. This island is a perfect landing spot if you want to get out of your boat and stretch your legs. Following a line of green cans, left, you enter deep water just south of the long finger of land, its tip fronted with riprap, that separates the two arms of Eel Pond. Now you are only a stone's throw from the salt pond on Washburn Island, and this is where you would take up the route description if you had portaged from there.

Making a gradual left-hand turn into the east arm of Eel Pond, you come to a heading of about 50 degrees and stay right of the main channel by keeping the red cans on your left. The familiar west shore of Washburn Island,

Salt-spray rose inhabits sand dunes, fields, and thickets

with its sandy beach, low dunes, and forest of pitch pines, is on your right. Soon you pass a point of land jutting out from the right that marks the end of Eel Pond. Now the channel narrows dramatically and you have the entrance to the Seapit River on your right and the Childs River ahead. Here you move to the left side of the Childs River, passing a public beach that may be crowded in summer with families and children. Even with an outgoing tide there is hardly any downstream current in this part of the river, and you may even be pushed upstream by a following breeze. Once past the Seapit River entrance, retrace your route to the launch site.

Chapter 8

Harwich

TRIP 12  HERRING RIVER

Length: 3.5 miles

Highlights

Cape Cod has countless tidal creeks and small streams but only a few rivers long enough to provide interesting paddle trips. Of these at least four are named Herring River—in Bourne, Eastham, Harwich and Wellfleet—for the herring-like fish called alewives that migrate up them in spring. This scenic route, best done as a shuttle trip, starts in West Reservoir, a flooded cedar swamp, and then descends the lazy, winding Herring River through the Cape's largest cattail marsh, past forests of pine and oak, and along vast tracts of salt marsh where bird life abounds.

Nearby attractions

Harwich has hundreds of acres of conservation lands bordering its ponds, lakes, and rivers, that are enjoyed by hiker, bikers, birders, and nature lovers. For information call the town offices, (508) 430-7513.

Tips

Launch around high tide for Nantucket Sound. If you are paddling solo, be sure you are adept at entering your unaided boat while it is floating in several feet of water, as it will be when you launch in the Herring River after crossing West Reservoir. If you are without a shuttle, you can do a short version of

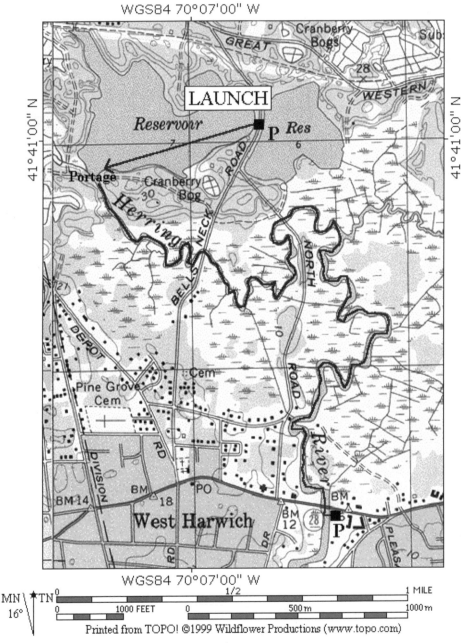

Trip 12—Herring River

this trip by landing just past the pedestrian bridge on North Rd. and walking back to the launch site to retrieve your car (see route description below for directions.)

Directions

This is a shuttle trip, starting at **West Reservoir** and ending at the **Herring River town landing** just south of Rt. 28 in West Harwich. Drive first to the town landing, leave a car there, and proceed to West Reservoir.

To reach the **Herring River town landing**: From Rt. 6 in Harwich, take Exit 10, signed for Rt. 124, Harwich, and Brewster. Follow Rt. 124 south toward Harwich and Harwichport. At 1.4 miles you reach a stop sign and a T-junction where Rt. 39 joins from the left. Turn right, then immediately left, and go another 1.3 miles to Rt. 28. Bear right and go 0.9 miles to a parking area and a town landing, left, on the east side of the Herring River.

To reach **West Reservoir**: Leave the parking area and turn left onto Rt. 28. Go 0.4 mile to Depot Rd. and turn right. After 0.1 mile veer right onto Bells Neck Rd. and go 1 mile to a clearing on the shoreline of West Reservoir, left.

Parking and facilities

Parking is available at the Herring River town landing and along the roadside at West Reservoir.

Launch

From the clearing on the west side of the road at West Reservoir.

Trip Description

West Reservoir, in the heart of Harwich's Herring Run Conservation Area, is a flooded cedar swamp, and you can see tree stumps which formerly stood on the pond's shore poking up above its murky surface. Here painted turtles soak up the sun on fallen logs, cormorants with outspread wings roost on stumps, and swans with young float gracefully around the shoreline. These are mute swans, and all members of this species on the Cape are descended from several pairs that escaped in the early 1900s from parks and estates in New York. Although beautiful to look at, mute swans are at the center of a debate among wildlife officials and nature lovers. Some want to control or remove the swans because they are an invasive species that may damage ecosystems and replace other waterfowl. Others want to accept the swans as being here to stay and let nature take her course.

The pond is a spawning ground for alewives, herring-like anadromous fish that swim in from Nantucket Sound and up the Herring River each spring. A flume, or fish ladder, located at the pond's southwest corner, aids their passage from the river to the pond, and a large culvert nearby drains excess water from the pond back into the river. Alewives have been an important food source on the Cape for thousands of years. In her wonderful book, *The Outer Lands*, Dorothy Sterling writes: "Netted by the thousands, the fish were fried, smoked or salted in tubs of brine, while any surplus went to fertilize hills of corn. The catch was so valuable that when a new dam in Falmouth blocked the passage of the fish a Herring Party and an Anti-Herring Party formed. During a protracted fight the Anti-Herrings filled a cannon on the village green with Alewives and fired it off, blowing fish, cannon and the man who fired it to bits."

Heading west from the launch site and weaving your way carefully through the tree stumps, some of which lurk just below the water's murky surface, you paddle parallel to the south shoreline, aiming for a landing spot just east of the culvert and the flume about 0.5 mile ahead. Along the shoreline grow such common Cape shrubs as sweet pepperbush, bayberry and swamp azalea, shaded by a forest of pitch pine, black oak, white oak, sassafras, and red maple. When you come to the first clearing on the left, land and drag your boat up a steep embankment about 50 feet to a dirt road. Here you turn right, go about 150 feet, and before reaching four wood pilings driven into the road descend left down a steep and narrow trail to the Herring River. (To view the flume leave your boat here and continue ahead about 100 feet.)

Once you reach the river you must float your boat, as there is no shoreline to launch from. A secure brace from a vertically held paddle resting on the river bottom is helpful here. Once comfortably settled in your boat again, you begin your descent of the river, with the culvert and flume on your right. The water here is brown, murky, and sluggish, and with a riot of trees, shrubs, marsh plants, and ferns hemming you in, the area resembles a fantastic Southern swamp, minus alligators. Your direction of travel is generally south, but the river has so many twists and turns that you will visit all points on the compass during this wonderful trip. Here the waterway is wide, several hundred feet across, and soon you enter the largest cattail marsh on Cape Cod, acres of the tall, cigar-tipped plants where almost nothing else grows. Canada geese are fond of this area, and you may see large families of them gliding on the river.

At a spot where the river widens and you are heading east—look for a house on the right and a stand of common reeds instead of cattails—you come to a junction. Straight ahead is a cattail island surrounded by a circular bulge in the river. You turn sharply right and then jog left, now with the Bells Neck Rd. bridge in view ahead. After paddling under it, and perhaps enjoying a shady respite, you follow the river as it pursues a winding course through a marsh of cattails, common reeds, and sedges. The blue water tower in the distance belongs to the town of Harwich and is useful as a landmark. If the tide is still coming in, you may begin to feel a slight current working against you from here on.

A second bridge, this one for pedestrians using North Rd. through the conservation area, comes into view for a moment, but you soon lose it as the river twists and turns. A circular expanse of river, with homes nestled in the trees to the left, may seem like a dead end, but you continue paddling northeast and then take an almost 180-degree bend to the left. Having left the cattails behind, you now have a salt marsh, low enough to look across for the first time, on your left, and a forest of tall pitch pines and black oaks on your right. Soon you have a clear view of the pedestrian bridge with the water tower lined up directly behind it. Just past the bridge on the left is a spot where you can land and get out of your boat. On foot from here it is less than 0.5 mile back to the launch site on West Reservoir, so if you have no shuttle you can end your trip here, haul your boat uphill to North Rd., and retrieve your car by turning right onto North Rd. and right again when you reach Bells Neck Rd.

Once past the bridge you come to a fork where you turn right toward the water tower. Now another right turn, this one sharp, has you heading south, but a horseshoe bend left swings you around to the northeast. To the left of your bow are houses on a bluff, and just to its right is the water tower. Yet another right turn brings you to a fork where you again stay right, avoiding a tributary of the river that heads east. Now the river resumes its generally southward course, and you should have the water tower behind you on your

Solitude greets visitor to the upper reaches of the Herring River

left. Here the river widens but remains snake-like, spinning you around the compass. The salt marsh here is home to many birds, including shorebirds such as spotted sandpipers and semipalmated plovers, and wading birds like great blue herons. Soon you begin to see traffic on Rt. 28 ahead in the distance, and now you paddle past homes and moored boats, signs of civilization. When you reach the bridge over Rt. 28, paddle under it and land at the boat ramp on your left.

TRIP 13  LONG POND

Length: 6 miles

Highlights

Who could resist a circumnavigation of the largest freshwater pond on Cape Cod? Ringed by a forest of oak and pine and bordered by some of the Cape's most lavish homes, the pond offers paddlers three separate lobes—west, north, and east—to explore, and two public beaches, not counting the one you launch from, on which to land. During fall, winter, and spring, the pond's waters are home to a variety of waterbirds, including loons, grebes, and ducks.

Nearby attractions

Brooks Academy Museum, operated by the Harwich Historical Society, has exhibits featuring the most important aspects of early Cape life, including seafaring and cranberry harvesting. Open June to October, the museum is located at 80 Parallel St. near the intersection of Rt. 124 and Rt. 39; (508) 432-8089.

Tips

In summer come early in the day to avoid crowds, and be prepared to encounter powerboats and jet skis.

Directions

From Rt. 6 eastbound in Harwich take Exit 11, signed for Rt. 137, Brewster, and Chatham. Turn right and follow Rt. 137 northwest 0.2 mile to Long Pond

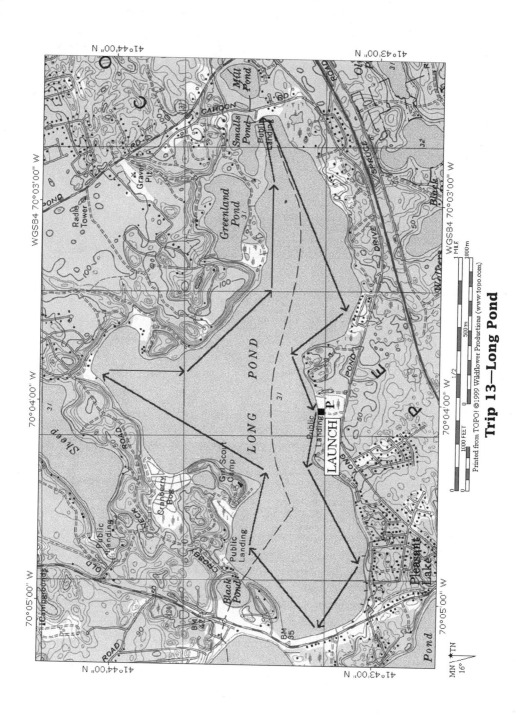

Trip 13—Long Pond

Dr. Turn left and go 1.8 miles to a road, right, leading to a beach and a town landing.

From Rt. 6 westbound in Harwich take Exit 11, signed for Rt. 137, Brewster, and Chatham. Turn right onto Rt. 137 and then immediately left onto Long Pond Dr. Go 1.8 miles to a road, right, leading to a beach and a town landing with a boat ramp.

Parking and facilities

A resident parking sticker is required from the last weekend in June through Labor Day. There are rest rooms here.

Launch

From the boat ramp or the beach adjacent to it.

Trip Description

This is the Cape's largest freshwater pond—743 acres, 66 feet maximum depth—and one of half a dozen or so on the Cape that carry the name Long Pond. Two towns divide ownership of the pond, Brewster getting the north half and Harwich the south. Powerboats, sailboats, jet skis, canoes, and kayaks all ply its waters, and just back from its shores sit spacious homes and manicured lawns. Your clockwise tour of the pond begins just west of a popular town beach with a swimming area marked by ropes and floats. As you leave the launch site on a heading of about 300 degrees, you paddle in shallow water over a rocky bottom and soon bear left around a point and into the circular west lobe of the pond. A forest of pitch pine and black oak is just back from the shoreline, and the water close to shore provides moorage for all types of pleasure craft.

You may see loons, grebes, and ducks on the pond, especially during fall, winter, and spring. Canada geese are here year-round. The Cape's extensive system of bays, harbors, salt marshes and ponds provides shelter for waterbirds throughout the year, and many species leave only briefly to breed in Canada and the Arctic. As you come close to the west shore, where most of the beaches are private, you begin to hear traffic noise from Hwy. 124, one of the main cross-Cape thoroughfares, connecting Brewster and Harwich. From here you can look east across the pond to get some idea of just how large it is. On your left, lavish homes decorate a bluff with a waterfront view. Ahead on a heading of about 60 degrees is a small public beach, ringed with ropes and buoys, wedged between private homes. This beach, in the town of Brewster, makes a good landing site if you want to get out of your boat.

Turning right, you soon pass a Girl Scout camp, where the beach may be strewn with sailboats, canoes, rowboats, and racks of life jackets. Now com-

Canada geese afloat on Long Pond

ing out of a cove and turning left around a rocky point, you begin paddling northeast on a heading of about 50 degrees into a more secluded lobe of the pond. The pine forest, left, offers fine perches for the belted kingfisher, one of the Cape's most colorful birds and a local nester. Kingfishers are common around ponds and streams, flying out from dense cover, hovering in midair, and then plunging into the water for fish. In Long Pond the menu includes bass, pickerel, and white perch. Behind a cove to your left, irrigated by water sprinklers, is a commercial cranberry bog, one of many on the Cape. Another cove, this one at the pond's extreme north end, provides more water to explore, and there is a sailing camp tucked away in the pine-and-oak forest behind its shores.

Long Pond in recent years has been plagued with a heavy bloom of algae resulting from high phosphorus levels, giving the water at times a blue-green sheen and resulting in fish kills. According to articles in *The Cape Codder*, the phosphorus comes from lawn fertilizers, septic systems, and storm-water runoff. Town officials in Brewster and Harwich are trying to come up with solutions to the problem, which could involve dredging, septic-system improvement, storm drainage within the watershed, development of natural buffer strips along the shoreline, and wastewater treatment within 300 feet of the lake. (When I visited in June of 1999, the water was murky throughout most of the pond but there was nothing at all unpleasant about paddling here.)

A heading of about 190 degrees takes you south back into the main part of the pond, and now you paddle southeast in shallow water, staying well off-shore to avoid the rocky bottom. This is a largely undeveloped side of the pond, with a fine forest of mostly deciduous trees. Keep a sharp eye and ear out here for powerboats and jet skis. Soon you pass the narrow barrier between Long Pond and one of its neighbors, Greenland Pond, to the north. From here the east lobe of the pond leads to a lovely public beach, just off Cahoon Rd., where you can land and stretch your legs. If you do not wish to land, you can turn south now and pick up the route description below. Once on the beach you have Smalls Pond, connected to Long Pond by a little stream, to your left. Along the shoreline nearby grow smooth alder, sweet pepperbush, and blueberry. Here also are picnic tables, a boat ramp, and a parking area (parking stickers required.)

Working your way southwest from the beach on a heading of about 260 degrees you come to within about 100 yards of the pond's south shore and then bear right to begin paddling parallel to it. Your goal is a point formed by a forested ridge extending north into the pond. Here the shoreline is rocky, evidence of the glacial moraine that formed this part of the Cape, and the forest is made up mostly of deciduous trees. Once around the point, where a house named Three Bears commands a fine view of the pond, you paddle almost due west toward the public beach you launched from earlier, which is about 0.25 mile ahead. In shallow water you skirt the roped-off swimming area, left, and then turn left toward the boat ramp and shore.

Chapter 9

Mashpee

TRIP 14  MASHPEE AND WAKEBY PONDS

Length: 8 miles

Highlights

This scenic circumnavigation of two ponds joined by a narrow waterway makes a great trip if you want to include picnicking and swimming on your day's agenda. Several fine beaches make inviting places to land and relax, but there is plenty to see on the water too, as the ponds are favorite hangouts for a variety of waterbirds and the forests surrounding them offer cover to many species of songbirds.

Nearby attractions

Lowell Holly Reservation is a 130-acre nature preserve on Conaumet Neck, the peninsula separating Mashpee and Wakeby ponds. The reservation, with picnic areas and 1.5 miles of hiking trails, is open from late May to mid-October, and features stands of American beech, holly, white pine, and rhododendron.

Tips

In summer come early in the day to avoid the crowds, and try to paddle during the week, not on weekends.

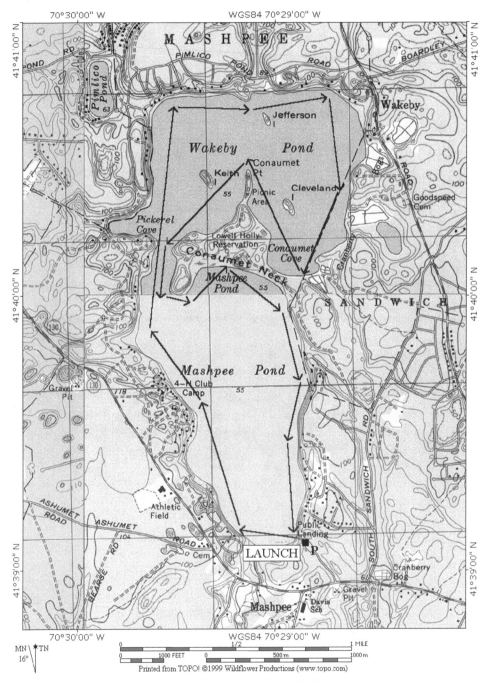

Trip 14—Mashpee and Wakeby Ponds

Directions

From Rt. 6 in Sandwich, take Exit 2, signed for Rt. 130, Sandwich, and Mashpee. Follow Rt. 130 south 7.4 miles to Fisherman's Dr., left, a poorly signed road that leads in a few hundred yards to a parking area and a boat ramp.

Parking and facilities

The free parking area and boat ramp are operated by the Massachusetts Public Access Board.

Launch

From the boat ramp downhill from and about 100 yards northwest of the parking area, or from the sandy beach just to the right of the ramp.

Trip Description

Two large ponds, Mashpee and Wakeby, joined by a narrow passage, constitute the Cape's second-largest body of freshwater, at 729 acres being just 14 acres smaller than Long Pond in Harwich (see previous trip). The town of Mashpee owns most of both ponds, but the town of Sandwich claims slivers of Wakeby Pond's east and west sides. Like most others on the Cape, these are kettle ponds, formed by the melting of huge buried blocks of ice left behind by the retreating glaciers. Mashpee is our deepest pond, besting Brewster's Cliff Pond by 1 foot. The pond and town take their name from the Indian words that mean "great water." The steep hillsides around the pond are heavily forested with deciduous trees, mostly black oak, white oak, and

Great black-backed gulls on Mashpee Pond

red maple, their limbs overhanging the water and their leaves rustling in the breeze. On the ponds in summer you are likely to see cormorants, Canada geese, mute swans, and several gulls, including great black-backed, ring-billed, and herring gulls.

Leaving the busy boat-ramp area, you turn left and paddle toward Mashpee Pond's west shore, beginning a clockwise circuit. You skirt a public beach, left, with a swimming area clearly marked by white-and-orange floats. These ponds are heavily used in summer by motorboats and jet skis, and the designated swimming areas are obviously off-limits to them. The powerboats seem to do most of their cruising though the middle of Mashpee Pond and in Wakeby Pond, so you can avoid them and have a thoroughly enjoyable paddle by staying close to the shoreline. There are many fine homes set on bluffs above the shoreline, and most have long wooden stairways leading down to wood or aluminum piers jutting into the pond with boats moored alongside. The clear water lets you see down to the pond's bottom, which is covered with stones and gravel, left behind by the glacier that formed the highlands north of here along Cape Cod Bay.

Passing a cove, left, and rounding a blunt point, you have Conaumet Neck, the peninsula that separates the two ponds, ahead to the north. On Conaumet Neck is the Lowell Holly Reservation, a 130-acre reservation donated in 1943 to the state by Harvard University president Abbott Lawrence Lowell. Soon you paddle by the 4-H Farley Outdoor Education Center, where an H-shaped wooden pier sits in the water, left, and ropes with floats mark a swimming

Boaters and swimmers enjoy Wakeby Pond from a beach on Conaumet Cove

area. In the woods just back from the water's edge are the camp's tidy cabins, and on shore you may see stacks of canoes and kayaks. Just past the camp, you begin to see pitch pines mixed with the deciduous trees, and this is a good place to drift slowly while watching and listening for birds. Common here are the eastern kingbird, a flycatcher, and the belted kingfisher, both local nesters. Kingfishers are year-round residents, but kingbirds, like so many who visit the Cape, depart for sunnier climes at the first hint of fall, returning in the spring.

Drifting close to shore also gives you an opportunity to do some botanizing, and in addition to the pines, oaks, and red maples you may find smooth alder, American beech, and swamp azalea with its lovely pale blossoms. As you near the narrows between Conaumet Neck and the west shore, you begin to see channel markers for the powerboats that ply these waters. Ahead is the wide and inviting expanse of Wakeby Pond, but while still in the narrows you move right to avoid the sandy shallows that reach out from shore. Once into Wakeby Pond, you have Pickerel Cove, a deep and narrow inlet, on your left. Here you can turn left to explore it or continue straight along the west shore of Wakeby Pond. Off to your right about 0.25 mile is Keith Island and just east of it is the narrow, north-pointing tip of Conaumet Neck.

Once you reach the northwest corner of Wakeby Pond and turn east, you paddle in deep water just a few hundred feet offshore. A few large homes on a hill dominate their immediate surroundings, but the lush, dense forest that begins just back from the pond's shoreline hides other abodes tucked away in the trees. Keith Island is now on your right, and it blends so well into the background of Conaumet Neck that the only clue to its separate identity comes from the motion of your boat. Ahead and slightly right of your bow is Jefferson Island. From the forest on the left you may hear the liquid whistle of the northern cardinal or the "teacher teacher teacher" cry of the ovenbird. As you near Wakeby's northeast corner you can see Cleveland Island, which used to be owned by President Grover Cleveland and used as a fishing and hunting retreat, in the distance to your right.

Turning south and paddling parallel to Wakeby's east shore you pass several cranberry bogs in low-lying areas wedged between Cotuit Rd. and the pond. Here the water is very shallow and the bottom rocky. Your goal is a beach on Conaumet Cove where you can land and get out of your boat. Your heading here is about 220 degrees. When you reach the cove, head for an opening between two roped-off swimming areas and land on the sandy shore. Here you will find covered picnic areas, rest rooms about 100 yards east, and in summer about noon each day, a Good Humor ice-cream truck. This is a fine spot for a picnic and a swim before you tackle the rest of the trip. From the shrubs near the beach you may hear the mewing of a gray catbird, and along the water's edge you may observe a spotted sandpiper flying with stiff wing beats.

After you have finished relaxing and enjoying the beach, launch your boat and head northwest to the tip of Conaumet Point, a very thin finger of land pointing north. Cleveland Island is to your right and Jefferson Island is ahead in the distance. Rounding the point, a densely forested peninsula ending in a shoal of rocks, you swing left and now have Keith Island, the third member of Wakeby's trio, on your right. (The sandy beach on the south side of Keith Island makes an inviting spot to land.) Continuing to the west side of Conaumet Neck and the narrows leading back to Mashpee Pond, you may find your progress noted by a snowy egret cruising overhead. Once in the narrows, you skirt a sandy shoal by moving right, and when you reach deeper water, turn left and paddle along the south side of Conaumet Neck. Venerable pitch pines tower over the hardwoods here, holdouts against the process of forest succession that, for now at least, seems to favor oaks and maples.

A secluded cove on the south side of Conaumet Neck, graced with a beautiful stretch of sandy beach, makes another fine picnic and swimming spot. Because this beach is part of the Lowell Holly Reservation, there is a small landing fee on Saturdays, Sundays, and holidays. Beneath the water's surface you see pond mussels on the bottom and schools of small fish gliding by. Now paddling south on a heading of about 190 degrees along Mashpee Pond's east shore, you pass a number of homes, piers, and moored boats, marking your return to a more populated area. As you near the launch site, stay well offshore to avoid rocky shoals on your left. Cutting across a cove where swimmers may be congregating on a raft, you reach the boat ramp and the sandy beach just to its left where you began this loop.

TRIP 15   POPPONESSET BAY AND THE MASHPEE RIVER

Length: 8 miles

Highlights

Variety is the spice of life, and this trip has a little of everything. Starting in sheltered Ockway Bay, you paddle in Popponesset Creek, Popponesset Bay, and the Mashpee River on a long but scenic semi-loop route that samples a wide variety of habitats. Along the way you visit a barrier beach where terns and shorebirds nest in summer, and a cattail marsh where great blue herons stalk their prey. If conditions are favorable, you can even paddle out to Nantucket Sound and have a picnic on a secluded stretch of white-sand beach.

Nearby attractions

Mashpee National Wildlife Refuge is a work-in-progress that links together already existing open space from Waquoit Bay to Mashpee and Wakeby ponds and hopes to acquire more. For more information, call The Friends of the Mashpee NWR, (508) 495-1702.

Tips

Launch two to three hours before high tide for Nantucket Sound.

Directions

From Rt. 6 in Barnstable take Exit 5, signed for Rt. 149, Marstons Mills, and W. Barnstable. Follow Rt. 149 southwest. At 1.4 miles you come to a roundabout, where you go half-way around and continue on Rt. 149. At 3.8 miles you bear right onto Rt. 28. Go 4.4 miles to the Mashpee rotary. Go three-quarters of the way around it to Great Neck Rd., signed for Popponesset. Go 2.5 miles to a paved road, left, just past Blue Castle Dr. on your right. Turn left and go about 100 yards to a town landing and a boat ramp.

Parking and facilities

Park in the Ockway Bay Boat Landing parking area just east of Great Neck Rd. and adjacent to the road to the boat ramp.

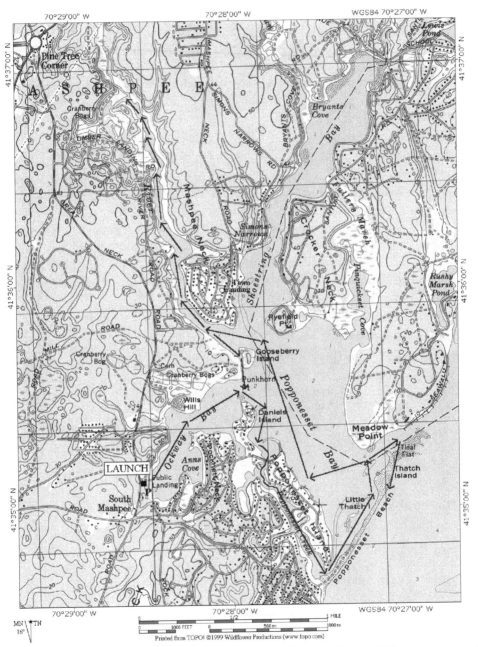

Trip 15—Popponesset Bay and the Mashpee River

Launch

From the boat ramp or the muddy beach next to it.

Trip Description

The protected harbor facing you is Ockway Bay, a narrow lobe of placid water surrounded on its shoreline by patches of salt marsh and, just back from the water's edge, a forest of pitch pine, black oak, eastern red cedar, black cherry and other common Cape trees and shrubs. After launching, you turn left and paddle northeast on a heading of about 40 degrees, with Anns Cove and Pockhett Neck on your right just across the water. There is an osprey-nesting platform on the shore of Anns Cove, and in summer you may see young in the nest and parents shuttling back and forth with meals of fish. Just past the tip of Pockhett Neck the bay widens considerably, and as you paddle by Wills Hill, left, you have a fine view of several glorious homes set on its heights. Now on a heading of about 75 degrees you aim for the narrows between Punkhorn Point, left, and Daniels Island, right, that marks the entrance to Popponesset Bay.

As you round the tip of Daniels Island, take a moment to get oriented, perhaps observed from its shoreline by a great black-backed gull or a great blue heron. Ahead of you stretches the expanse of Popponesset Bay, almost completely sealed off from Nantucket Sound by Popponesset Beach, a barrier of shore and low dunes. The bay opens to the sound through an inlet between the tip of Popponesset Beach, called Thatch Island, and Meadow Point. To your north are Punkhorn Point and Gooseberry Island, separated from the mainland by a narrow passage. Across from Gooseberry Island to the northeast is Ryefield Point, a protuberance jutting southwest from Crocker Neck. Northwest of Gooseberry Island is the entrance to the Mashpee River, and north of Ryefield Point is Shoestring Bay.

Now that you've gotten the lay of the land—and the water—turn right and paddle in shallows along the shoreline, skirting piers and moored boats. Your goal is the entrance to Popponesset Creek, a narrow body of water spanned by a bridge that allows vehicle access to Popponesset Island. A heading of about 180 degrees puts you in line for the bridge and creek, but you may be distracted by the magnificent homes on Daniels Island, right. Once under the bridge you have the New Seabury Marina on your right and a fork ahead where you stay left. Continuing south in Popponesset Creek, you pass a residential area on the island, left, with homes built in a variety of styles, some looking more like mountain chalets than waterfront cottages. Canada geese are at home here, floating between the piers and the moored boats.

Soon you reach the back side of Popponesset Beach. Here the creek narrows, turns sharply left around the southeast tip of Popponesset Island, and then in about 100 yards flows into Popponesset Bay. If you want to get out of your boat you can land on the sandy beach ahead before making the left-hand turn. From the beach an opening in the low dunes leads south to a vantage point overlooking Nantucket Sound. Once back in the water, you paddle the hundred yards or so to Popponesset Bay, which is quite shallow at this end and obstructed directly ahead by a small sandbar called Little Thatch Island. If you have enough water, you can continue northeast on a heading of about 40 degrees and pass between the sandbar and the strand of Popponesset Beach to your right. If it is too shallow, paddle left around the bar into deeper water near the main channel, indicated by red and green markers.

Popponesset Beach, a bird sanctuary, is roped off in summer to protect nesting terns and shorebirds. You can land here but you must not walk across the dunes, where the birds have their nests and young. The northeast tip of Popponesset Island is called Thatch Island, and like many "islands" on Cape Cod the shifting sands and swirling waters have, perhaps only temporarily, connected it to the mainland. Beyond Thatch Island is the passageway to Nantucket Sound, which just skirts Meadow Point to the north. If conditions are favorable—slack tide, calm winds, low seas—you can venture out into the sound and paddle southwest along the outer beach, a beautiful and often deserted stretch of sand and low dunes. Here you may find sanderlings, shorebirds that breed in the high Arctic and winter along both US coasts.

Kayak class, Ockway Bay

Described in birding guides as resembling clockwork toys, sanderlings run to and fro with the waves, probing with their bills in the damp sand for food.

Once back inside Popponesset Bay, you head west away from the main channel and cross shallow water on a heading of about 270 degrees. There is deeper water ahead near Popponesset Island. When you reach it you turn right and paddle past Daniels Island and the mouth of Ockway Bay, working your way north on a heading of about 350 degrees toward Gooseberry Island. The island is ringed with salt marsh, cloaked with groves of black oak and a few pines, and in summer decorated with the lovely red and white blooms of salt-spray roses. (If you want to shorten the trip by omitting the Mashpee River, you can turn left into Ockway Bay before reaching Gooseberry Island and then retrace you route to the launch site.)

Once past Gooseberry Island you have the option of continuing straight to a town landing at the end of Mashpee Neck Rd. and getting out of your boat, or swinging left into the mouth of the Mashpee River. If you go to the town landing, simply retrace your route to the mouth of the river and turn right. Once in the river, feeling perhaps a slight assist from the tide if it is still rising, you have on your right Mashpee Neck, a peninsula thickly settled with homes, some of which front the river. On the left is a sparsely settled area between the river and Great Neck Rd., and west of the road are the South Mashpee Pine Barrens, more than 300 acres of pine groves and rare Atlantic white-cedar swamps, all part of the Mashpee National Wildlife Refuge.

In the summer of 1999, some residents along the Mashpee River—which drains Mashpee and Wakeby ponds—began displaying signs in their yard protesting pollution in the river. Many of the signs read MASHPEE OUTFALL CANAL, an ironic reference to the controversial outfall pipe from Boston that carries wastewater into Cape Cod Bay. There were notices posted at the town landings warning people not to eat shellfish caught in the surrounding waters, and one neighbor displayed a sign with a skull and cross-bones. Several other Cape towns are experiencing water-pollution problems, and with a limited aquifer and increasing development the problem is going to get worse unless a solution is found.

As you get farther up the river, where the flushing action of the tide is weak, its color changes to a chocolate brown and you begin to see stands of cattails, plants indicative of brackish water. A bulge in the river resembles a small pond, and the tall pines and oaks here offer perfect habitat for the belted kingfisher, a year-round resident and local nester. Marshlands bordering the river provide cover for great blue herons and other wading birds. This is a very picturesque area if you enjoy being removed from any evidence of civilization. Soon you paddle past a small landing spot and a bench in the shade of the trees, both right. Ahead you have pure stands of cattails in a large marsh similar to one on the Herring River in Harwich. Marsh wrens, small birds with surprising loud, scolding voices, make their nests in these cattails. The river branches here, with an arm veering left and another going straight, and this makes a good turn-around point. Now retrace you route to the mouth of the river.

With Gooseberry Island dead ahead on a bearing of about 140 degrees, you paddle toward the narrow passage between it and the mainland, which may be hidden until you get close. Bearing right into the passage, you glide past Gooseberry Island, left. At high tide you have about 3 feet of water here, and swinging right around Punkhorn Point you return at last to Ockway Bay. Now retrace your route past Pockhett Neck and Anns Cove to the launch site.

Popponesset Beach separates Nantucket Sound, left, from Popponesset Bay

Chapter 10

Orleans

TRIP 16　LITTLE PLEASANT BAY

Length: 7 miles

Highlights

Little Pleasant Bay, the north end of a large inland waterway that includes Chatham Harbor and Pleasant Bay, is one of the best places to paddle on Cape Cod. Numerous coves, islands, creeks, and rivers provide hours of enjoyable exploration, and the salt marshes on the bay's east edge, part of Cape Cod National Seashore, are home to a wide variety of birds, including nesting ospreys. This semi-loop trip, which includes a circuit of Sampson Island, starts at the upper reaches of The River and passes through Hog Island and Broad creeks on its scenic tour of Little Pleasant Bay.

Nearby attractions

Cape Cod National Seashore's Salt Pond visitor center is just east of Rt. 6 in Eastham about 3 miles north of the Orleans/Eastham rotary; (508) 255-3421. Fort Hill, the Penniman House, and the Red Maple Swamp are reached via Gov. Prence and Fort Hill roads, east of Rt. 6. about 1.5 miles north of the rotary. The south end of Nauset Marsh is best experienced by water, as described in the following trip.

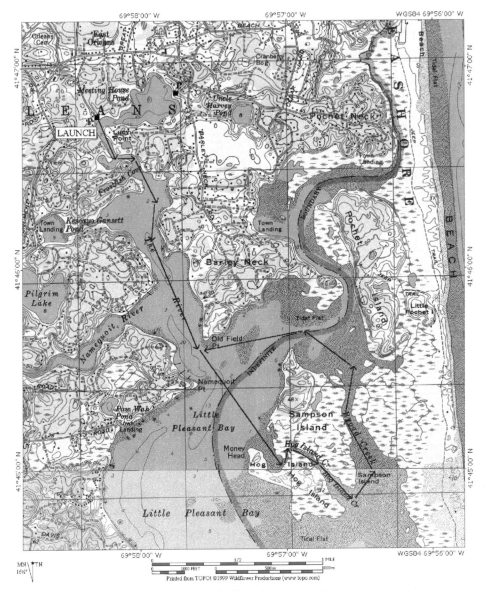

Trip 16—Little Pleasant Bay

Tips

Launch two to three hours before high tide for Meetinghouse Pond, which occurs about 1 hour 45 minutes later than high tide for the Atlantic shore.

Directions

From the Rt. 6 rotary at the Eastham-Orleans line, follow Rt. 6A/28 south 0.5 mile to a fork where Rt. 28, signed for Chatham and Falmouth, branches left. Bear left, go 0.4 mile to a traffic signal at Main St. and turn left. After 0.5 mile you veer right onto River Rd. Go several hundred feet to a stop sign at School Rd. (caution: this is not a four-way stop). Continue straight on River Rd., signed for a town landing. Go 0.4 mile to a parking area and a boat ramp at the end of River Rd.

If this parking area is full, you can launch from Meetinghouse Pond, about 0.5 mile east. Return to School Rd., turn right, go several hundred feet to Main St. and turn right again. Go 0.7 mile to a fork where Beach Rd. goes left and Barley Neck Rd. goes right. Go right and go 0.2 mile to another fork. Here Pochet Rd. goes straight and Barley Neck Rd. goes right. Turn right, go 0.3 mile, and turn right into a parking area for a public beach and a boat ramp.

Parking and facilities

Park in the small parking area adjacent to the boat ramp.

Launch

From the boat ramp.

Kayaker enjoys paddling The River near Meetinghouse Pond

Trip Description

As you leave the boat ramp and turn right, you enter a busy waterway called The River, which connects Meetinghouse Pond, left about 0.5 mile, with Frostfish Cove and Little Pleasant Bay. Passenger and freight vessels from New York working their way up from Chatham Harbor used to land here in bygone days, but now you are likely to be accompanied by sailboats, powerboats, canoes, and other kayaks. On July 4th weekend, The Friends of Meetinghouse Pond holds a regatta here with hundreds of paddlers. The main channel runs down the middle of The River, and you stay just to its right. A breeze blowing up-river and the tidal current may be working against you here. Just across from the boat ramp is Lucy Point, and soon after paddling past it you come to a T-junction where you turn left. Now a right turn takes you past an inlet, right, and then you enter Frostfish Cove. On your right is another inlet, this one leading to Kescayogansett Pond, where there is another town landing.

The land on your left now is Barley Neck, part of East Orleans and one of the loveliest residential areas on the lower Cape, graced with fine stands of evergreen and deciduous trees. Once in Frostfish Cove, carefully cross the main channel, left, and then exit the cove by paddling south along the west shore of Barley Neck, giving wide berth to a rocky point ahead. A small cove just to its east makes a convenient spot to land and get out of your boat, as there will be few other opportunities ahead. The water here, and throughout much of Little Pleasant Bay, is shallow even near high tide, so the powerboats are restricted generally to the main channel. This is one of the reasons the bay is so popular with sailors, canoers, and kayakers. Across the water to your right is the wide mouth of the Namequoit River, a winding and shallow passage to Areys Pond and another town landing.

The end of Barley Neck at Old Field Point marks the entrance to Little Pleasant Bay. To your right is Namequoit Point, to the left is a channel for boats coming down the east side of Barley Neck, and ahead are Sampson and Hog islands and the creek between them that is your immediate goal. Old Field Point is very rocky, so use caution when passing it. Ahead are three channel markers, one red can and two green ones. On a heading of about 180 degrees, keep the red can on your right and paddle across open water toward Hog Island, the southernmost of the two. This crossing in shallow water can be exciting if there is a stiff breeze from the south, because it doesn't take much wind to whip up small waves and whitecaps. Holding your course, you soon come to a protected cove ringed with salt marsh between Sampson and Hog islands. You are now in Cape Cod National Seashore, the boundary of which encompasses the two islands here, Pochet Island to the northeast, and the long strand of Nauset Beach to the east.

This area is one of the few places on the Cape where ospreys nest in close proximity to each other. Three nesting platforms are positioned nearby, two on Hog Island and one on Sampson. This is an interesting area to explore, especially if you are a birder, and you may be joined here by other watercraft, including a commercial tour boat that around high tide brings visitors to view the nesting ospreys. One of the osprey nests on Hog Island is just south of Money Head, a promontory jutting north. To find Hog Island Creek, the waterway that separates the two islands, paddle toward Hog Island, and as you near its shore turn left into a broad tidal creek. Soon the creek swings right and you have an expanse of salt marsh on your left bordering Sampson Island. Look here for the second osprey-nesting platform and resist the urge to approach too close if it is occupied. The third nesting platform is on Hog Island, ahead and to your right. A long finger of salt marsh extends southeast from Hog Island, which is surrounded by very shallow tidal flats.

After passing the third nesting platform you begin a left-hand turn to paddle up the east side of Sampson Island. Broken only by Broad Creek, which empties as the tide falls, the vast salt marsh here extends from Sampson Island all the way across to the dunes on the back side of Nauset Beach, a barrier beach that extends south from Orleans to Chatham. On a heading of almost due north, and paddling several hundred feet offshore, you have

Osprey nest, Hog Island Creek, Sampson Island

Pochet Island just right of your bow at about 1 o'clock and the high ground of Barley Neck on the skyline behind Sampson Island. As you work your way through Broad Creek you soon come to an area that may be crowded with shellfishing rigs, including buoys floating on the surface and nets on the shallow bottom. Stay well clear of these and continue north into open water between Sampson Island, Pochet Island, and Barley Neck.

Now turning left on a heading of about 280 degrees and watching for boat traffic, you aim for a white tower on the skyline ridge to the west. This will put you in line for Old Field Point at the tip of Barley Neck. A sheltered cove just northeast of the point makes a good place to land, although the beach is somewhat rocky. Look here for green herons, diminutive cousins of the great blue, as they stalk through the salt marsh. If you choose to land in this lovely area, you will find some of the Cape's common salt-marsh plants, including saltwater cordgrass, glasswort, and sea lavender growing along the water's edge. Just back from the shore, which is littered with large boulders and rocks left behind by the glaciers, grow eastern red cedar, black oak, bayberry, and salt-spray roses. Now keeping well off Old Field Point you turn right, paddle into The River, and retrace your route to the launch site.

TRIP 17   TOWN COVE TO NAUSET BEACH

Length: 4.5 miles

Highlights

This route, a shuttle trip, leaves Town Cove and heads northeast to the south end of beautiful Nauset Marsh, a vast waterway full of salt-marsh islands and teeming with bird life, part of Cape Cod National Seashore. You also get to visit scenic Nauset Harbor, once open to the Atlantic but now silted in and embraced by an arm of Nauset Beach. Landing on the back side of the beach, you have the opportunity to enjoy the Atlantic shore for swimming, picnicking, and relaxing.

Nearby attractions

The north end of Nauset Marsh can be visited by following the route description for "Nauset Marsh" elsewhere in this guide.

Trip 17—Town Cove to Nauset Beach

Tips

Timing is not critical, but if you want plenty of water launch about 2 hours before high tide for Town Cove, or about the time of high tide for the Atlantic shore.

Directions

This is a shuttle trip, starting at **Town Cove** and ending at **Mill Pond**. Drive first to Mill Pond, leave a car there, and proceed to Town Cove.

To reach **Mill Pond**: From the Orleans/Eastham rotary on Rt. 6, follow Rt. 6A/28 south 0.3 mile to a traffic signal at the entrance to Stop and Shop, right. Continue straight another 0.2 mile to a fork where Rt. 28, signed for Chatham and Falmouth, branches left. Bear left, go 0.4 mile to a traffic signal at Main St. and turn left. Go 0.2 mile to a traffic signal at Tonset Rd., turn left and go 0.5 mile to Hopkins Rd., right, just past the cemetery. Veer right and go 1 mile to a stop sign where Brick Hill Rd. goes sharply right and also left. Bear left, go 0.3 mile to a fork, and bear right onto Champlain Rd. Go 0.2 mile to Mill Pond Rd., turn right and follow it 0.5 mile through several right-angle bends to a parking area and a town landing on Mill Pond.

To reach **Town Cove**: Retrace your route to the traffic signal at Stop and Shop. Turn right and go 0.1 mile to a boat ramp and parking area, right.

Parking and facilities

There is a large public parking area on Town Cove. Just north of the parking area is the Goose Hummock Outdoor Center, one of the Cape's premier paddle-sport outfitters. Here you will find boat sales and rentals, lessons, guided trips, maps, books, and lots of helpful advice. Toilets are available late spring through early fall. There is a small parking area on Mill Pond.

Launch

From the boat ramp between the parking area and the Goose Hummock Outdoor Center.

Trip Description

As you leave the boat ramp and paddle into Town Cove, you are in a busy boat moorage, with the Goose Hummock's pier on your left and the Jonathan Young windmill, vintage 1720, on a bluff to your right. Paddling east across the cove on a heading of about 90 degrees and crossing the main channel, you soon reach the southeast shore and turn left. Here the cove is about 0.5 mile wide, but as you head northeast toward Nauset Marsh it narrows considerably. Passing Rocky Point, a rampart guarding an array of fine homes perched on a hill, you work you way toward Hopkins Island on a heading of about 40 degrees. Most of the cove is shallow, and the main channel swings around the west side of Hopkins Island. If there is enough water, and there should be if you timed your launch correctly, you can pass around the island's east side by staying right as you approach it. Green markers on your left before the island will confirm that you are out of the channel.

Kayak class, Goose Hummock Outdoor Center

As you paddle through the narrows east of Hopkins Island, you have a cove on your right, and here your route dog-legs right and then resumes its heading of about 40 degrees. Once past the island you again have the boat channel immediately on your left. A narrow inlet, right, leads to Rachel Cove, a salt pond you might wish to explore. Eastham's waterfront, hidden from motorists on busy Rt. 6, presents a vista of fine homes across the cove on your left. Once past Rachel Cove, you begin to catch glimpses of Nauset Marsh, its low salt-marsh islands, and perhaps even the old Coast Guard Station perched above Nauset Bay ahead in the distance. To the left of your bow at about 11 o'clock is the Fort Hill area, part of Cape Cod National Seashore and certainly worth a visit.

Turning right and rounding Snow Point, you find safe passage on a heading of about 145 degrees between offshore rocks, right, and the main channel, left. The colored floats here during summer are lobster buoys, and you will see many of them as you work your way toward Nauset Harbor. According to *The North Atlantic Coast*, a Sierra Club guide, American lobsters can live up to 100 years, grow to 4 feet in length, and weigh up to 45 pounds. Most lobsters, however, are caught as soon as they reach legal minimum size. Lobstering began around 1800 in Cape Cod and then spread to Maine and Canada. Near shore, lobsters are caught using fish heads and other types of bait in traps that rest on the bottom of shallow bays and harbors. Because lobsters migrate farther offshore in winter, most lobstermen pull their traps out of the water in late fall.

To your left is the low and narrow form of Stony Island, almost indistinguishable from the large salt-marsh island behind it. A passageway on the west side of the island, behind you and left, leads past Fort Hill and Skiff Hill to Hemenway Landing, a popular powerboat launch site. In deep water now and passing through a boat moorage, you paddle by the entrance to Woods Cove, right, steering clear of a red-and-white buoy marked ROCK on your left. Beyond the entrance to Woods Cove is a point, right, and off it are more rocks, so use caution. The middle of Nauset Harbor, ahead, is shallow and filled with sandbars, but there is deep water near shore. Turning right and paddling parallel to the shoreline on a heading of about 220 degrees you soon reach another boat moorage and a town landing, right, where a lovely beach invites you to land.

After landing and stretching your legs, walk up the set of wooden steps that lead to the parking area for a wonderful scenic overview of Nauset Harbor. The beach here makes a fine spot for a brief respite from paddling, but you will have an opportunity later to enjoy Nauset Beach and the Atlantic Ocean, so you may want to save your main out-of-boat activities, such as swimming and picnicking, for then. Launching from the beach and turning right, you soon pass Snow Shore Landing, famous locally for being the site in 1979 of a large drug bust involving bales of marijuana brought in by ship. Picture the scene here as it was on that impenetrably foggy night, with shadowy figures moving silently back and forth from sea to shore and then the sudden and blinding glare of police searchlights. As you approach the landing you turn left and paddle through the boat moorage, staying several hundred feet offshore to avoid submerged rocks.

A heading of about 140 degrees takes you past a cove fringed with salt marsh, right, and then past the inlet, also right, to Mill Pond, which you will visit later at the end of your trip. For now, paddle past the inlet and then skirt a public beach, right, on your way around the tip of Nauset Heights. Ahead is the low sandy barrier of Nauset Beach, and beyond it, the Atlantic Ocean. Not too long ago this was a true harbor, with an inlet from the ocean. Over time, however, sand deposited by shore currents gradually choked off the inlet and silted in the harbor, but pounding surf widened another inlet farther north, and that is the one used now by boats. The effect has been to turn Nauset Harbor into a shallow, quiet cove, perfect for paddling. This will undoubtedly change in the future, as currents and wave action seal off old inlets and create new ones. Following the shoreline as it wraps to the right, you work your way to the southeast corner of the cove, moving left to avoid a rock jetty and several submerged rocks. A steep bluff, right, is crowned with beautiful homes.

On your left is the back side of Nauset Beach, a long spit of sand that runs south from here uninterrupted to Chatham, part of Cape Cod National Seashore. Here you can land and spend some time enjoying beautiful vistas of the open ocean and the seemingly endless line of sloping sands washed by breakers. A short path leads through the low dunes from your landing site to the outer beach. Four-wheel-drive vehicles are allowed on Nauset Beach with seasonal closures to safeguard nesting least terns, common terns, and piping plovers, all three protected species. Dogs are not allowed on the beach during summer months. Once you are ready to continue, launch and retrace your route to the inlet leading to Mill Pond. Here you turn left and on a heading of about 210 degrees paddle toward a narrow gap between a peninsula pointing

View of Nauset Harbor from town landing

southeast, right, and a hook of land guarding a cove, left. Rounding the peninsula and turning right into Mill Pond, you head west and soon reach a town landing, right, above which is the parking area with your shuttle vehicle.

Jonathan Young windmill (1720) overlooks Town Cove

Chapter 11

Provincetown

TRIP 18  PROVINCETOWN HARBOR AND LONG POINT

Length: 4 miles

Highlights

This scenic loop tour of Provincetown Harbor cruises along the waterfront and then visits Long Point, the sandy tip of Cape Cod, where two picturesque lighthouses stand guard and miles of open beach beckon visitors to enjoy walking, swimming, fishing, picnicking, and birding. If conditions are favorable, adventurous paddlers can round the tip of Long Point and explore Cape Cod Bay.

Nearby attractions

Cape Cod National Seashore's Province Lands visitor center, open April through November, is on Race Point Rd. a little more than a mile northwest of the traffic signal at Rt. 6. Check here for information about area beaches, hiking trails, and bike paths; (508) 487-1256. The Pilgrim Monument and the Provincetown Museum, in the center of town, feature exhibits on the Pilgrims and Cape Cod life, plus a fantastic view earned by climbing to the top of the monument; (508) 487-1310.

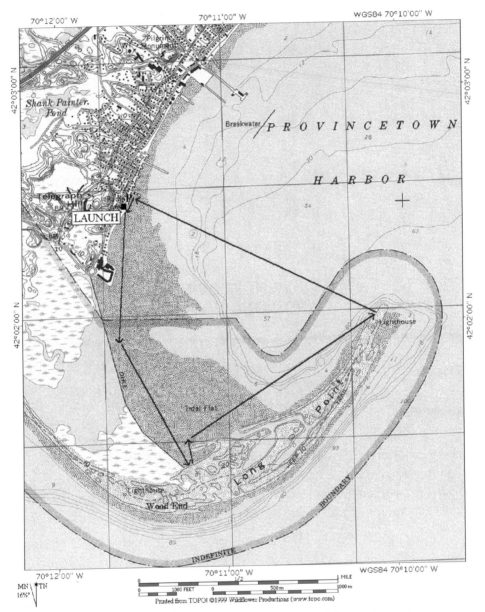

Trip 18—Provincetown Harbor and Long Point

Tips

Launch about an hour before high tide for Provincetown Harbor. In summer avoid weekends and plan to arrive before 8 A.M. to get parking. Bring plenty of insect repellent to discourage gnats and mosquitoes.

Directions

On Rt. 6 in Provincetown go 0.5 mile past the traffic signal at Conwell St., signed for Provincetown Center (left), Race Point and Provincelands Visitor Center (right), to a flashing yellow light at Shank Painter Rd., signed for Rt. 6A and Provincetown. Turn left, go 0.5 mile to Bradford St., and turn right. Go 0.2 mile to Franklin St. and turn left. Go 0.1 mile to a stop sign where Commercial St. goes left and also straight. Go straight and then follow Commercial St. as it jogs right. After 0.2 mile you reach a parking area and a boat ramp, left.

Parking and facilities

Parking here is metered, and you get 30 minutes for each quarter (bring plenty). In summer the parking area fills early each morning; on-street parking is difficult to find and may involve a long walk.

Launch

From the boat ramp or from the sandy beach to its right.

Trip Description

After launching, paddle out through a boat moorage and then take a moment to get oriented. Provincetown, the fist at the end of the Cape's "bared and bended arm," has a busy central district and two residential areas flanking it, the East and West ends. You are in the West End, a (relatively) quiet residential area with picturesque waterfront homes, many of them built on pilings and extending out over the water. Across the harbor to the southeast is Long Point, the very tip of Cape Cod. As you face Long Point, the large wharf on your left is the Coast Guard wharf. Beyond it is the central district marked by the Pilgrim Monument, a 250-foot granite tower that commemorates the Pilgrims' first landfall in the new world, and by MacMillan Wharf, the landing and departure point for fishing boats, tour boats, whale-watching cruises, and various ferries that shuttle visitors to and from Plymouth and Boston. The East End, with many shops, restaurants, and art galleries, is beyond the central district to your left.

You turn right and paddle toward the dike, a mile-long rock structure that separates Provincetown Harbor from a large salt marsh to its west. A favorite pastime of visitors and locals alike is to walk along the dike from the end of Commercial St. all the way out to its terminus on Long Point. Two lighthouses grace Long Point, one at Wood End just west of the dike, and the other at the tip of Long Point. The area just east of the dike is a vast mudflat that is exposed at low tide. As you paddle southwest on a heading of about 210 degrees, you have a great view of the closely packed homes that line the waterfront, most of them sporting weathered gray shingles and white trim. Behind them on a bluff overlooking Commercial St. and the harbor are examples of more modern architecture, some of them quite elaborate and lavish. Two landmarks on your right are the Red Inn and past it the much larger Provincetown Inn. Next to the Provincetown Inn at the end of Commercial St. is Pilgrims' First Landing Park, another reminder that it was here, and not in Plymouth, that the Pilgrims first landed.

After you pass the Provincetown Inn you begin to turn left and paddle southeast on a heading of about 170 degrees parallel to the dike. The water in this part of the harbor is normally very clear, and you may catch a glimpse of fish swimming past your boat. As you approach Long Point and move into shallower water, you may hear the mournful note of the foghorn at Wood End Light. Both Long Point Light (1826) and Wood End Light (1873) are square rather than circular, an unusual design for the Cape. If you want to go ashore and walk through the dunes to Cape Cod Bay you can do so by landing at Long Point on a beach just left of the dike. Be sure to pull your boat up to the beach grass and well past the high-tide line. The large flat-topped boulders that form the dike continue inland, and you can use them as a pathway. After about 100 yards the dike ends and you continue southeast on a path through the dunes. Among the plants growing here are poison ivy, bayberry, beach plum, and huge circular clumps of salt-spray rose hunkered down in the dunes.

Back in your boat now, you leave the beach and work your way east, paddling in shallow water and skirting an area of salt marsh on its left. Now on a heading of about 75 degrees, you aim for Long Point Light a little more than a mile ahead. From here you have a fine view across the harbor to the

Kayak class in Provincetown Harbor with the Pilgrim Monument in the background

Provincetown waterfront and the Pilgrim Monument, modeled after a tower in Sienna, Italy. In the distance, off your bow at about 11 o'clock, are the Province Lands dunes, part of Cape Cod National Seashore. You can visit the dunes on ranger-led walks and learn more about their formation and the hearty plants and animals that thrive there. Some of the dunes carry biblical names, including Mt. Ararat, just north of Rt. 6 on the Provincetown/Truro line, for the mountain where Noah's ark came to rest after the flood. In these sand-swept hills and gullies are the locally famous dune shacks, which in the past were refuges for such artists and writers as Norman Mailer, Jackson Pollack, Eugene O'Neill, Jack Kerouac, and e. e. cummings. Some of the shacks are now preserved and administered by the Peaked Hill Trust, whose members enter a lottery to win temporary stays in them. For more information write the trust at PO Box 1705, Provincetown, MA 02657. The Peaked Hill Bars off Provincetown's back shore claimed many vessels on their way around the Cape.

As you near Long Point Light you may hear its solemn foghorn warning mariners to steer clear. In fact, large boats like the ferries and the whale-watching vessels stay well offshore, but fishing boats, powerboats, and sail-boats may cut close to the point. In summer boats may be moored along the harbor side of Long Point, and on the beach people may be sunbathing and picnicking. The sandy strand near the lighthouse invites you to land, or if conditions are favorable you can continue around the tip of Long Point into Cape Cod Bay. Use caution when rounding the point and move quickly past it, as the wake from passing boats causes surf to break on the shore and confusing swells to form. There may be people fishing from the point, and you must stay clear of their lines. The large green can ahead and left is the channel marker for large vessels, and they pass outside of it on their way to and from MacMillan Wharf.

If you land near the lighthouse on the harbor side, pull your boat well up from the water, as wakes from passing boats could float yours. The lighthouse is set back about 100 yards from the tip of Long Point, which consists of a low sandy flat and a mound with a clump of beach grass. Just southwest of the lighthouse is a hill topped with a cross and a tattered American flag. A path leads from the beach up the hill, and this makes a fine vantage point from which to survey the tip of Cape Cod. The flag and cross are a memorial to one Charles S. Darby, killed in World War II. The brick fuel shed between the hill and the lighthouse is a roost for gulls, and its shingled roof is plastered with their droppings. Two plants of interest here are winged sumac, related in name only to poison sumac, and pokeweed, a rank shrub with red stalks and clusters of berries that turn black in early autumn.

As you leave the beach on your return trip across the harbor, watch for swimmers, water skiers, powerboats, and jet skis. A heading of about 320 degrees will take you across deep water to the Coast Guard wharf, and your launch site is about 0.25 mile to its left. As you near the wharf you paddle through a boat moorage and a shellfishing area. On your right is the breakwater that sits off MacMillan wharf, unique in that it runs parallel rather than at right angles to the shoreline. If you want to extend your trip, you can turn left and paddle under the Coast Guard Wharf and along the shoreline toward MacMillan Wharf, perhaps stopping at a waterfront restaurant for lunch. Otherwise, turn left on a heading of about 225 degrees and enjoy one last look at the homes along the shoreline before reaching the boat ramp and your launch site.

Long Point Light and WWII memorial

Chapter 12

Sandwich

TRIP 19  **SCORTON CREEK**

Length: 6 miles

Highlights

This adventurous out-and-back route starts about midway on Scorton Creek, a scenic tidal waterway with many tributaries that connects a large salt-marsh system with Cape Cod Bay. The opportunity to bird, botanize, and even fly-cast for striped bass or sea-run brown trout from your kayak are all reasons to enjoy this trip.

Nearby attractions

Heritage Plantation, just north of Rt. 6 on Grove and Pine Streets, has 76 acres devoted to gardens and a museum of Americana, including antique cars and firearms. Heritage Plantation is open Mother's Day through mid-October; (508) 888-3300. The nearby Sandwich Glass Museum, open April through October, is famous for its extensive collection of 19th century glassware; (508) 888-0251. Shawme-Crowell State Forest off Rt. 6 offers overnight camping. For information call (508) 888-0351; reservations (877) 422-6762.

Tips

Launch several hours before high tide for Cape Cod Bay. Use caution when nearing the mouth of the creek at Scorton Harbor—there is a strong current on an outgoing tide that can sweep you through standing waves into Cape

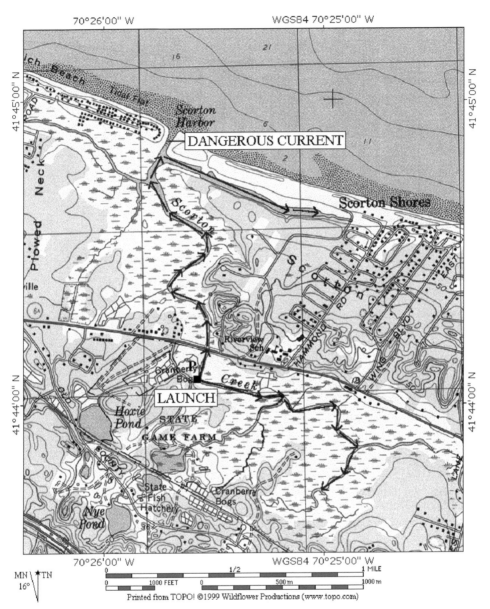

Trip 19—Scorton Creek

Cod Bay. Be prepared to paddle against the tidal current on the leg from Scorton Harbor back to your launch site.

Directions

From Rt. 6 in Sandwich take Exit 4, signed for Chase Rd., and go north 0.5 mile to Old County Rd. Turn left and go 1.8 miles to Rt. 6A. Turn right, go 0.6 mile, and just before the bridge over Scorton Creek turn right onto a paved (barely!) road and go 0.2 mile to a parking area, left.

Parking and facilities

Parking is in a dirt area beside the creek.

Launch

From the muddy creek bank just north of the parking area.

Trip Description

Scorton Creek is a scenic ribbon of water that twists and turns its way from Cape Cod Bay through a large salt marsh wedged between the shoreline, Rt. 6A, and the old Penn Central railroad tracks. At the launch site the creek is deep and the bank steep except at high tide, when water reaches the salt marsh a few feet below the parking area. As you launch and head upriver the creek turns east and you may not even have to paddle if the tide is still rising. The area around the launch site is popular for fishing, and you may even see people fly-casting from kayaks. The water here, cleansed twice daily by the tides, is clear and cold. Behind the salt marsh bordering the creek are stands of pitch pine and black oak. The state once ran a game farm just south of here that raised pheasant and quail for hunting, but it is now closed and awaiting reincarnation perhaps as a nature preserve.

An osprey-nesting platform, right, rises over a broad expanse of salt marsh made up mostly of salt hay in matted tufts, punctuated here and there by clusters of sea lavender and marsh elder. This is a fine habitat for birds, and you may spot great blue herons, green herons, spotted sandpipers, and least sandpipers as you paddle by. A vast area of salt marshes, called the Great Marshes, once stretched unbroken from Barnstable Harbor west to where the Cape Cod Canal now joins Cape Cod Bay. The salt hay that grew in these marshes provided fodder for the early settlers' animals, and after harvesting it was carried to dry land in wagons pulled by horses or oxen wearing wooden "bog shoes" to negotiate the mud. Passing a wooden pier extending toward you on your left, you follow the creek as it bends gently right.

When you come to a fork, stay left and parallel to Rt. 6A. The many blue boxes here in the marsh are traps for greenhead flies, summer pests that inflict painful bites. The flies seek the shade provided by the boxes, which have an opening on their undersides. Once inside the trap the flies cannot escape and are doomed. The farther up the creek you go, the murkier and more sluggish the water becomes as the tidal influence lessens. When you reach a T-junction where the creek splits into two narrow arms, you have the option of exploring more or turning around. Growing here is freshwater cordgrass (*Spartina pectinata*), a tall marsh grass related to saltwater cordgrass (*Spartina alterniflora*). When you have finished exploring the marshlands along the upper reaches of Scorton Creek, retrace your route to the launch site.

Passing the launch site, you now follow the creek as it swings right and heads north toward Rt. 6A. Paddling under a bridge, where swimmers may be diving into the creek, you begin to see the closely packed homes that line the sandy spit west of Scorton Harbor, which is merely an inlet from Cape Cod Bay. The bayside beach west of the harbor is usually called Springhill Beach but appears on the USGS map as East Sandwich Beach. Few other

Kayaker in Scorton Creek near launch site

Kayaker in Scorton Creek paddles under the Route 6A bridge

beachfront areas on the Cape have cottages this close together. Soon the creek, crystal clear and with a sandy bottom, begins to wind its way northwest toward Scorton Harbor. On your right is more salt marsh, and on your left a beautiful woodland encloses a handful of homes. Look here for an osprey-nesting platform on your left, and scan the skies for terns, both common and lesser. You may also see and hear both greater and lesser yellowlegs as they fly over the marsh. Greater yellowlegs generally give a three-to-five syllable "tu-tu-tu" call, whereas lesser yellowlegs, smaller and daintier birds, commonly have a one- or two-syllable call.

Saltwater fly-fishing for striped bass is beginning to catch on in Cape waters, and kayaks make good platforms for this endeavor. You may see people pursuing these elusive fish in this stretch of the creek. Striped bass are classified as semi-anadromous, meaning they mature at sea and return part way up brackish estuaries to spawn. Conservation efforts have helped increase the numbers of this once-declining species. As you near the creek mouth, you pass a tributary, left, that runs northwest through the salt marsh bordering Plowed Neck. Boats may be moored here, and there is a landing on your left. Another tributary goes southeast just before Scorton Creek empties into Cape Cod Bay through a narrow, rock-lined, potentially dangerous inlet. On an outgoing tide, a strong current runs through the inlet, and standing waves form where the rushing waters run over shallow tidal flats at the mouth of Scorton Harbor. You can easily find yourself swept out into Cape Cod Bay with no way to get back into the creek until the tide changes.

If you want to land and get out of your boat, you can do so on the west side of the creek opposite the tributary that heads southeast. From here you can walk along the rock jetties that line the inlet at the mouth of Scorton Creek and view Cape Cod Bay. To explore the tributary heading southeast, paddle across to its mouth—remembering to compensate for tidal current, a technique called ferrying—and mosey upstream past the remnant of an old bridge toward a housing development called Scorton Shores. On your right is a barrier beach topped with low dunes. On your right are homes on a bluff, screened by shrubbery. The clear and sandy-bottomed creek narrows as you wend your way upstream between lovely islands of salt marsh, paddling until you run out of water. Now turn around and retrace your route to the launch site.

Chapter 13

Truro

TRIP 20  PAMET RIVER AND HARBOR

Length: 5 miles

Highlights

This delightful out-and-back tour, centered around picturesque Pamet Harbor, explores the lovely Pamet and Little Pamet rivers and then samples a bit of Cape Cod Bay. Bordered by acres of salt marsh, the rivers are perfect for paddling or just drifting with the tide, whereas Cape Cod Bay beckons more experienced and adventurous kayakers with miles of open water and sandy, dune-backed shoreline. Picnicking, swimming, strolling, and lounging can all be added to the agenda. A day spent here, doing as much or as little as you want, is truly rewarding.

Nearby attractions

Cape Cod Light, also called Highland Light, casts its far-reaching beacon from a high bluff above the Atlantic Ocean a little more than 3 miles north of Pamet Harbor. Constructed in 1797, rebuilt in 1853, automated in 1986, and moved back from an eroding dune in 1996, the lighthouse offers daily tours from mid-May through October; (508) 487-1121.

Tips

Launch several hours before high tide for Cape Cod Bay. In summer avoid weekends and come early to get a parking space.

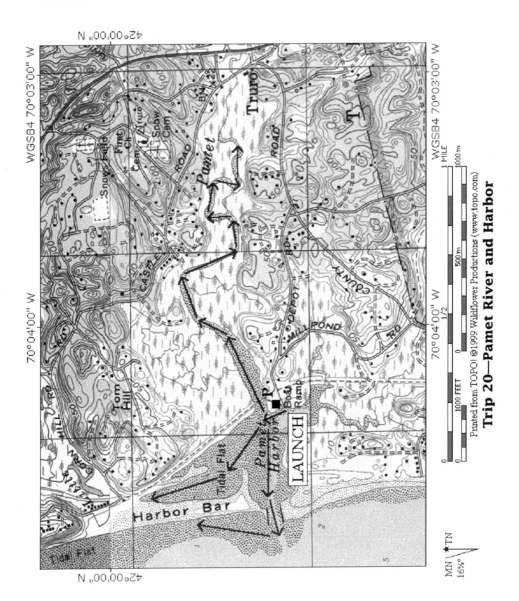

Trip 20—Pamet River and Harbor

Directions

From Rt. 6 northbound in Truro take the exit signed for Pamet Roads and Truro Center. After exiting, you come to a junction signed for North and South Pamet roads. Turn right, go several hundred feet, and turn right onto South Pamet Rd. which goes under Rt. 6. After 0.1 mile you come to Castle Rd. Turn left, go about 100 feet and veer right onto Depot Rd. After 0.5 mile the road forks and you stay right toward Pamet Harbor. At 1.3 miles you come to the harbor parking area and twin boat ramps.

From Rt. 6 southbound in Truro take the exit signed for Pamet Roads and Truro Center. After exiting go 0.1 mile to Depot Rd. and turn sharply left. After 0.5 mile the road forks and you stay right toward Pamet Harbor. At 1.3 miles you come to the harbor parking area and twin boat ramps.

Parking and facilities

The parking area and boat ramps are operated by the Massachusetts Public Access Board. From the beginning of May through the beginning of October there is a small fee for parking and boat launching. Use is free during the rest of the year. There is a toilet on the south side of the parking area.

Launch

From one of the two side-by-side boat ramps or, if you can carry your boat down a flight of stairs, from the beach behind the harbormaster's shack on the west side of the parking area.

Trip Description

This busy little harbor is one of the best places from which to launch a kayak, because you have access not only to the Pamet and Little Pamet rivers but also to Cape Cod Bay. The only drawback is that the harbor is crowded during the summer with powerboats and sailboats all vying to be first into the bay. The two rivers, however, are used mostly by non-motorized craft and they offer some of the most pleasant and relaxed paddling on the Cape. The Pamet River actually gets its start about 2.5 miles northeast as the crow flies, in a wetland tucked behind the dunes that rise from the Atlantic shore. It is divided almost exactly in half by Rt. 6, but manages with help from culverts to work its way under the highway and other roads. The upper reaches of the river, wedged between North and South Pamet roads, are narrow and over-grown. Tidal influence is felt from the harbor inland toward Rt. 6 but as it weakens, the river changes from a crystal-clear waterway to a sluggish, debris-laden, chocolate-brown stream.

Leaving the launch site you turn right and thread your way carefully through the assembly of moored boats, skirting the parking area on its west side. Once past the parking area you turn right on a heading of about 80 degrees. This is the entrance to the Pamet River, and a combination of an incoming tide and a breeze from Cape Cod Bay may help push you upstream. Here the river is bordered by large tracts of salt marsh, flooded around high tide. Behind the marshes rise the sandy bluffs and wooded hills that give Truro, a sleepy town beloved by its residents and loyal summer visitors, its special character. Paddling or perhaps drifting with the incoming tide, you follow the wide river as it bends left and then pass around either side of a salt-marsh island. A right turn puts you back on a heading of about 80 degrees, with the broadest expanse of salt marsh on your right. You may notice blue wooden boxes on legs set in the marsh. These are traps for green-head flies, which can become bothersome in July, especially when the weather is hot and humid. As the river narrows, the effect of the tidal current is magnified, aiding you in your efforts. Along the way you may see two unrelated birds—least terns and belted kingfishers—whose hunting styles, hovering and diving for fish, are remarkably similar.

The river now swings southeast and you approach the shore where a white boathouse stands at the foot of a low sandy ridge studded with pines. A kink in the river sends you eastward, and as you cruise through the marsh you can examine two of our most common salt-marsh grasses—saltwater cordgrass, in low areas where it is drenched twice-daily by the tide, and salt hay, growing higher in the marsh and often forming large meadows of matted tufts. About 100 yards past the boathouse the river jogs left, and now you begin to shuttle back and forth between the north and south sides of the river valley. Another salt-marsh island can be passed on either side. An apparent cul-de-sac may have you momentarily stymied, but a sharp right-hand turn that aims you temporarily southwest provides a way out. As you near Rt. 6 the river widens for a short stretch but then hems you in with stands of freshwater cordgrass and common reed. Your passage through this swampy area may be noted and protested by red-winged blackbirds, local nesters that are very territorial. Where the river becomes murky and debris-laden, turn around and retrace your route to Pamet Harbor.

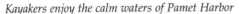

Kayakers enjoy the calm waters of Pamet Harbor

Once back to the harbor with the parking area to your left, paddle on a heading of about 270 degrees, passing low dunes, rocks, and pilings on your right. Avoid the main channel, which is left, and keep a sharp eye out for a rocky reef marked with orange buoys that is submerged at high tide. Your goal is the Little Pamet River, which flows through a salt marsh tucked just behind Harbor Bar, also called Gull Island. The harbor here is a work-in-progress, with constant dredging required to keep it open. The location of the inlet to the harbor from Cape Cod Bay used to move with the passing seasons, shifting as far north as Corn Hill, but rock jetties built by the state in the 1950s have anchored its position. One result of this engineering, however, has been to increase siltation in the harbor as sand drifts back toward the Pamet River during the winter.

To explore the Little Pamet River, when you are past the rocky reef turn right on a heading of about 335 degrees into its wide mouth, which soon narrows to a tidal creek passable only around high tide. To continue instead to Harbor Bar and a landing spot, paddle west past the mouth of the Little Pamet River to a point where the inlet from Cape Cod Bay squeezes to its narrowest width—here you have the main channel immediately on your left. Just ahead is a cove, right, at the foot of the north jetty. The cove has a rocky bottom but a sandy beach that makes a fine landing spot. Be sure to pull your boat well up from the waterline, as wakes from passing boats could easily float yours. Cape Cod Bay and a beautiful beach are just several hundred feet west. Here you can enjoy a picnic, a swim, or perhaps a stroll on the beach. You can also evaluate conditions in the bay in case you want to paddle out of the harbor into open water. The dunes to your right are protected nesting areas for terns and piping plovers.

If you choose to go through the inlet from Cape Cod Bay, do so on a slack tide. As water drains from the two rivers and the harbor, a swift current begins to run through the inlet and out to the bay. This could cause you problems, especially when you try to return to the harbor. If conditions are favorable, launch from the cove described above and turn right, paddling along the north jetty and watching for boat traffic. You may get confused swells here as water sloshes back and forth between the north and south jetties. In summer the prevailing afternoon wind is usually from the southwest, and this can push swells toward the mouth of the inlet. When you reach the end of the north jetty and are clear of any submerged rocks, turn sharply right to avoid a sandbar that may be lurking a few hundred feet off its tip. Move close to shore and turn left, paddling parallel to the beach. If you spotted a least tern earlier, compare it with the common terns you are likely to see along the shore. Adult least terns are slightly smaller than robins and have a black cap, a yellow bill, and yellow legs. Common terns are about 50% larger and have a black cap, an orange bill, and red legs.

The high ground to the north with a town landing at its base is Corn Hill, so named because it was here that the Pilgrims on their first exploration ashore found baskets of Indian corn, took all they could carry, and came back a few weeks later for second helpings. Although this act of thievery helped save the Pilgrims from starvation, it also sadly symbolizes the beginning of a generally unequal relationship between settlers and Native Americans that continued from this time forward. Truro also provided the Pilgrims with their first taste of freshwater, from a spring near High Head, and some of the party wanted to settle here. Another group, under the command of Myles Standish, decided to make a more complete exploration of the coastline in a small boat, and after much hardship, including the loss of mast and rudder, washed up in Plymouth Harbor. After you have finished reflecting on the human and natural history that makes the Cape such a vibrant and provocative place, retrace your route into Pamet Harbor to the launch site.

Kayaker on Pamet River near Pamet Harbor

Chapter 14

Wellfleet

TRIP 21  DUCK CREEK

Length: 3.5 miles

Highlights

This out-and-back route past the Wellfleet marina and into Duck Creek is a scenic journey back in time, because the mouth of the creek was once a busy harbor and the waterfront, now lined with art galleries and inns, bustled with activity. The creek winds its way under an old wooden bridge and into a salt marsh, and here you lose most hints of human activity and instead experience nature on an intimate scale as you paddle by.

Nearby attractions

Don't miss Wellfleet's wonderful art galleries, especially the Left Bank Gallery on Commercial St., and nearby restaurants such as Aesop's Tables on Main St. For the best ice cream on the Cape, check out A Nice Cream Shop on Main St. just west of Aesop's. The Wellfleet Library on West Main St. has a wonderful collection of books about the Cape's human and natural history, along with plenty of books by Cape authors.

Tips

Launch about one hour before high tide for Wellfleet Harbor. Bring insect repellent to ward off gnats and mosquitoes.

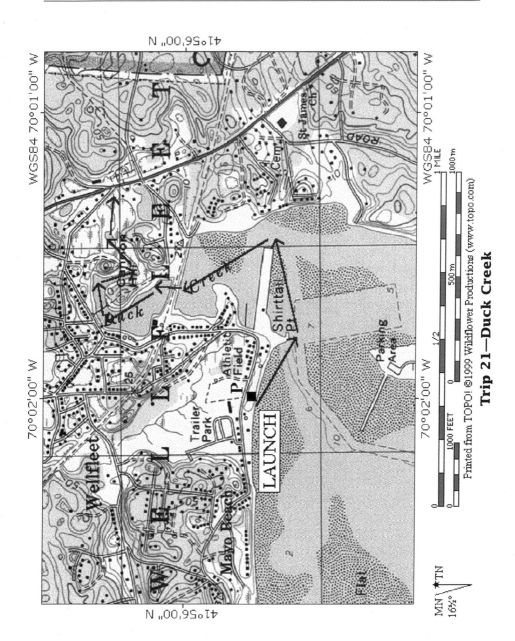

Directions

From Rt. 6 in Wellfleet at the southernmost traffic signal, take the exit signed for Wellfleet Center and Harbor. This puts you on Main St., which you follow west for 0.3 mile to E. Commercial St. Turn left and follow E. Commercial St., which soon becomes Commercial St. Go 0.7 mile to the town marina and harbor. Turn right onto Kendrick Ave. and after several hundred feet veer left into a parking area.

Parking and facilities

Park on either the east or the west end of the parking area to find paths to the beach. There are toilets nearby and a restaurant across Kendrick Ave.

Launch

From the sandy beach just south of the parking area and outside of the roped-off swimming area. Use the existing paths to access the beach and do not put boats on the grass around the parking area.

Trip Description

As you launch into the protected waters of Wellfleet Harbor, take a moment to get oriented. The marina and boot moorage are left, busy in summer with the coming and going of pleasure craft, fishing vessels, wind surfers, canoers, and other kayakers. Directly south across the harbor is Indian Neck and the rock jetty that serves as a breakwater, helping to guard the harbor from southwest swells. Because most of the harbor is shallow even at high tide, and almost without water at low, boats follow a narrow, dredged channel from the marina out to the breakwater and beyond. The stretch of beach extending right is called Mayo Beach. To the southwest loom Great Island and Great Beach Hill, part of Cape Cod National Seashore, two of four former islands that march south from the Wellfleet/Truro line. Connected to each other and to the mainland by low, sandy strands called tombolos, they form a peninsula that divides Wellfleet Harbor and Cape Cod Bay.

Turning left on a heading of about 140 degrees, you paddle carefully past a small rock jetty, left, and then skirt a pier where fishing boats may be docked. When you reach the pier's east end use caution and listen for engine noise, as you may not be able to see vessels coming out of the inner harbor, left, until they are upon you. The main channel, right, is indicated by red and green markers. Mariners returning to port keep the red markers on their right—"red, right, returning"—and the green ones on their left. If you keep the green markers on your right you will be out of the channel. As you paddle through the boat moorage on a heading of about 90 degrees, you have the marina's side-by-side boat ramps and a parking area on Shirttail Point, left. If it is windy, the craft moored here will be swinging around their single mooring lines, creating what can be a dizzying and disorienting maze of moving boats.

Coming to the end of Shirttail Point, you squeeze between its rocky tip, left, and the main channel, right. The north side of the point is lined with docking slips for boats of all shapes and sizes, from small sailboats to large cabin cruisers. Wait until there are no vessels entering or leaving this area, and then paddle north on a heading of about 340 degrees across a wide cove, actually the mouth of Duck Creek, which at low tide is a vast mudflat. Ahead above the trees rises the First Congregational Church tower, from whose heights bells ring out indicating ship's time, reportedly the only town clock in the world to do so. You tell ship's time as follows: two bells for 1, 5, and 9 o'clock; four bells for 2, 6, and 10 o'clock; six bells for 3, 7, and 11 o'clock; and eight bells for 4, 8, and 12 o'clock. An extra bell indicates the appropriate half hour.

Wellfleeters have always been intimately connected with the sea, whether roaming the world to hunt whales, plying the offshore Atlantic waters for mackerel and cod, or searching local sandbars and mudflats for oysters and clams. Historically, this cove—the mouth of Duck Creek—was one of the

Kayaker paddles past boats moored at Wellfleet Marina

Duck Creek flows under Uncle Tim's Bridge

town's three harbors, and Commercial St. to your left bustled with activity as schooners tied up alongside piers to load and unload. Wellfleet's connection with the sea and the bodies of water within its bounds continues today, as tourists flock here in summer to enjoy swimming, boating, surfing, and fishing. *Sports Afield* magazine in 1999 named Wellfleet one of the top 50 towns in the US for outdoor sports, specifically citing kayaking and saltwater fishing.

As you cross the cove, you have ahead a dike and the remnant of a bridge, built in 1869 to accommodate the Old Colony Railroad tracks which ran through Wellfleet and on to Provincetown. After rail service was discontinued, part of the railroad right-of-way was turned into a bike route called the Cape Cod Rail Trail, which now runs from the town of Dennis all the way to Wellfleet. Turning right to paddle through a gap in the dike once spanned by the railroad bridge, you now veer left into a lovely cove dotted with islands of salt marsh, some barely visible at high tide. Cannon Hill is the sandy, pine-studded rise on your right and Uncle Tim's Bridge is ahead on a bearing of about 20 degrees. Both are venerable Wellfleet landmarks. Cannons fired from atop hills on the Cape announced the arrival of packet boats, and Wellfleet's Cannon Hill is one of three with that name on the Cape. The town's Fourth-of-July fireworks used to be launched from the hill but now are fired more safely from a barge in the harbor. Behind the bridge rises the church tower, completing this picturesque scene.

Now you paddle under the bridge and then after about 100 yards turn right, keeping Cannon Hill on your right. Ahead the creek forks around an island and you stay right. At the next fork you veer left on a heading of about 130 degrees. The muddy banks beside the creek are home to fiddler crabs, and you may see them standing by their burrows or scuttling into them as you pass by. Male fiddler crabs have one small claw and one large one which they wave to attract females and ward off competitors. As the creek narrows, it meanders through the salt marsh, and if the tide is still rising you may be able to drift upstream without paddling. Given a choice, keep to the widest channels, and when you reach an apparent cul-de-sac—a house with a brick chimney and a deck will be ahead—make an almost-180-degree turn to the right to find your way out. A short boat is definitely an advantage here, and a rudder comes in handy for quick turns.

As you near Rt. 6 the creek widens for a short stretch and then narrows, forcing you to hold your paddle almost vertically. Another technique that comes in handy is to get up speed where the creek is wide enough to paddle normally and then hold your paddle parallel to your boat and steer by dipping the rear-facing blade in the water. Unless the tide is at full flood you may

Family kayak trip begins from Wellfleet Marina

not be able to make it all the way to Rt. 6, but if you do you'll find a wide spot to turn around.

Now retrace your route to the launch site. From here to Uncle Tim's Bridge it is easy to stray into a side channel or a backwater. If the tide is still rising, you can watch debris floating upstream to help determine the correct channel. As an aid to navigation, keep the house with the brick chimney and deck, and two others nearby, on your left. As you pass these houses aim for Cannon Hill on a heading of about 290 degrees. The church tower should be right of your bow at about 2 o'clock.

TRIP 22  GREAT ISLAND

Length: 7 miles

Highlights

One of the Cape's favorite paddle destinations is the glacially molded peninsula, part of Cape Cod National Seashore, that separates Wellfleet Harbor from Cape Cod Bay. On this wonderful semi-loop route you paddle across the busy harbor and then enter a wilderness of shoreline and salt marsh where humans come to visit but do not remain. Take a picnic, a novel, and a beach towel and you have the makings of a wonderful, relaxing day.

Nearby attractions

Cape Cod National Seashore's Great Island Trail, which starts about 2.5 miles west of the town marina near the intersection of Chequessett Neck and Griffin Island roads, is a 7-to-8 mile (round-trip) route through pine forests, beside salt marshes, and along the narrow spit between Wellfleet Harbor and Cape Cod Bay.

Tips

Launch two to three hours before high tide for Wellfleet Harbor. Bring binoculars for birding.

Directions

Same as for previous trip.

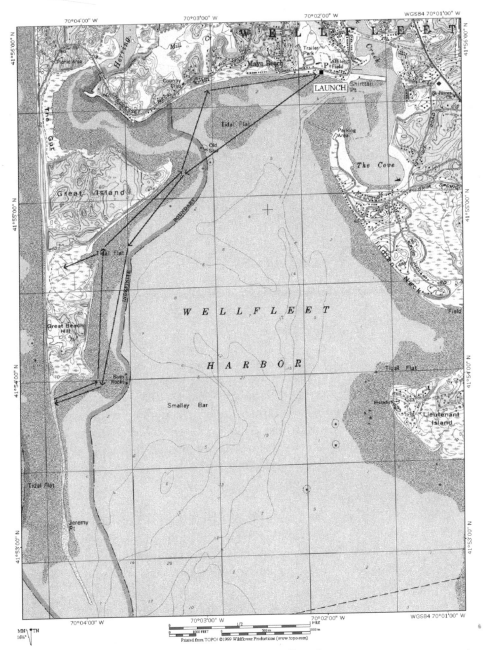

Trip 22—Great Island

Parking and facilities

Same as for previous trip.

Launch

Same as for previous trip.

Trip Description

As you launch from the sandy beach, you are in the protected waters of Wellfleet Harbor. You have the town pier and marina on your left, the main channel marked with red and green cans ahead, and the hulking peninsula of Great Island and its neighbor to the south, Great Beach Hill, in the distance to your right. Extending south from Great Beach Hill is Jeremy Point, and beyond that, barely visible at low tide, is a sandbar called Billingsgate Shoal, once the site of a thriving community but now abandoned to the sea. This peninsula forms the divide between Wellfleet Harbor and Cape Cod Bay. Great Island and Great Beach Hill, part of Cape Cod National Seashore, are two in a set of four former islands running south from the Wellfleet/Truro line, the other two being Bound Brook and Griffin islands. Over many years, erosion and shore drifting created sandy strands called tombolos that connected the islands to each other and to the mainland. The beachfront to your right is called Mayo Beach and along its shore in summer may be a multitude

A sea kayak is a sleek and stable craft

of swimmers, sailboats, powerboats, wind surfers, canoers, and other kayakers.

You turn right and paddle on a heading of about 250 degrees across the harbor, steering clear of the numerous commercial shellfish beds, marked with floats, that dot the tidal flats and shallows close to shore. In summer the prevailing wind is from the southwest, and it usually kicks up in the afternoon. The harbor, although protected by the landmass to the west, is open to the south, and it is not unusual to get small waves and even whitecaps here. Powerboats passing by can also cause wakes and swells. As you paddle along Mayo Beach, look right to see some wonderful homes set back from the water's edge. A lighthouse used to stand just west of the parking area, and the keeper's house, flanked by a small brick fuel house, is still there, square with steeply pitched gables on each side. Farther west is a large beachfront house with an elaborate turret, known locally as the Elephant House.

Off Mayo Beach is a large tidal flat, and after you have been paddling for 10 or 15 minutes you may be surprised to see bottom again after having lost sight of it just offshore. In fact, much of Wellfleet Harbor is so shallow that when the tide is extremely low, around the time of the new and full moons, you can almost walk across it. Your route passes by several rocks, one called Old Saw on the USGS map. These are exposed as the tide falls but may be lurking just under the surface at other times. Other hazards to watch for

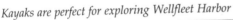

Kayaks are perfect for exploring Wellfleet Harbor

Visitors to Great Island enjoy a picnic on the beach

include boats pulling water skiers and commercial fishing trawlers dragging gear behind them. Assume you are invisible to them and stay out of their way. As you approach Great Island, you have a large cove on your right. This is actually the mouth of the Herring River, a stream that collects the waters of four ponds east of Rt. 6 near the Atlantic shore. One of Wellfleet's original harbors was in the mouth of the river.

As you come within several hundred yards of Great Island's east tip, you may see people walking along the beach but no boats in sight. A popular hiking trail (see **Nearby attractions** above) leaves from the south side of Griffin Island and takes visitors to the Jeremy Point overlook at the end of Great Beach Hill. One branch of the trail leads to the site of a tavern that may once have stood somewhere on the east side of Great Island. The tavern is said to have been a retreat for whalemen in search of whiskey and women. In 1970, archeologists digging on Great Island found thousands of artifacts and the foundation of a building which they say was in use from 1690 to 1740. Was this the tavern of local legend? No one knows for sure, and there are no visible remains of the site today. From the 17th century forward, Wellfleeters made their living from the sea, whether by whaling, fishing, or shellfishing. Even today, it is the surrounding waters—Wellfleet Harbor, Cape Cod Bay, the Atlantic Ocean, and the town's freshwater ponds—that draw visitors and keep the town economically afloat. Much of the town's waterfront property, along with a large part of its marshes, dunes, and pine forests, is protected from further development by being in the national seashore.

Turning left on a heading of about 220 degrees, you paddle parallel to the shoreline for a short distance, keeping a sharp eye out for an offshore rock. As the beach swings away to the right, you hold your course to pass well offshore of a cove at the entrance to a salt marsh, sometimes called Middle Marsh, which you will visit later. In early summer, the waters here may be teeming with young striped bass, moving in schools and chasing bait fish. The pine-topped high ground of Great Island, right, blocks the prevailing summer winds and also your view of approaching weather. A sudden squall can blow in from Cape Cod Bay without much warning, so pay particular attention to the weather forecast, especially if afternoon thunderstorms are predicted. Even without a storm, dead calm here can be replaced in a few minutes with a stiff breeze as you move to less sheltered water farther south.

As you draw abreast of Great Beach Hill look for a small cove, right, and then a sand spit ahead. If you are close to shore, move well off to round the spit. Smalley Bar extends east from the spit, and the water here may be very shallow, even near high tide. Small wavelets may form over the bar if it is windy. Once past the bar, you turn right and paddle into a large cove fringed with salt marsh. During breeding and nesting season you may begin to hear the cries of terns as they soar overhead. Other birds that collect in the marsh and on the nearby beach include gulls and shorebirds, and the low dunes pro-

Middle Marsh, Great Island, Cape Cod National Seashore

vide nesting areas for threatened piping plovers. On your left, the narrow finger of Jeremy Point, devoid of vegetation, extends well to the south, a magnet for pleasure craft during summer. The cove you are in has a sandy beach that makes a fine landing spot, but take care not to disturb roosting or nesting birds. When you get out of your boat and explore on foot, please respect all posted closures. If the tide is still rising and you plan to venture out of sight of your boat, be sure to pull it well up from the waterline and past the wrack line.

A low, beach-grass-covered dune and a bit of beach on either side here are all that separate Wellfleet Harbor from Cape Cod Bay. Just north is the Jeremy Point overlook and the terminus of the Great Island Trail. If you walk over to the bayside shoreline and the visibility is good, you can probably pick out the Pilgrim Monument in Provincetown, a dozen or so miles to the northwest. During spring and fall migrations, the beach here is a great place to search for shorebirds such as semipalmated sandpipers, semipalmated plovers, sanderlings, ruddy turnstones, whimbrels, and greater yellowlegs. After you have finished relaxing and enjoying this remote and wild area, launch into the cove and retrace your route across Smalley Bar. (If you want to extend your trip, you can do so by paddling south along Jeremy Point, but use caution when approaching its tip because a strong current runs around it and across the shoals extending south.)

Once across Smalley Bar hug the shoreline and follow it north on a heading of about 20 degrees, aided perhaps by a following breeze, to the cove that affords entrance to Middle Marsh. This cove is guarded by a sand spit that juts north, so you will have to paddle past its tip and then turn hard to the left. Once inside the cove, you are facing a large salt marsh with numerous islands and channels. If the tide is high the marsh will be flooded, with just the upper stalks of the saltwater cordgrass above water. You can follow the channels, some of which connect with each other, almost all the way to the tombolo that links Great Island and Great Beach Hill. At higher elevations in the marsh, the cordgrass is replaced by salt hay growing in large meadows. Salt hay (*Spartina patens*) was a valuable crop for many years on the Cape. Early settlers harvested the hay and used it as fodder for their animals. This is a beautiful area to explore, but be prepared to do some backward paddling in case you reach a dead-end channel and cannot turn around. You may be lucky enough to see an osprey winging its way over the marsh and out to the harbor to dive for fish. There are even a few sandy beaches here where you can land and climb a low rise to survey the marsh. When you have finished exploring, retrace your route to the harbor.

From here you paddle parallel to the shoreline on a heading of about 70 degrees. When you reach the east tip of Great Island veer slightly left on a heading of about 40 degrees, watching for boat traffic as you cross the mouth of the Herring River. If the wind is up you may be able to ride low swells all the way to the opposite shore. To the left of your bow is the Wellfleet Country Club, and dead ahead is a beach named Powers Landing but known locally as Seashells, after the cottages immediately to its west. This landing has a medium-sized parking area but requires a beach sticker in summer. Be especially careful to watch for swimmers and boat traffic as you approach the beach. When you are about 100 yards offshore, you turn right on a heading of about 100 degrees and paddle parallel to the shoreline, passing the Elephant House and then a concrete retaining wall which at extreme high tide may reflect waves back into the harbor, creating confusing swells. Mayo Beach, ahead, has a number of rock jetties extending south several hundred feet into the water, so give them wide berth. Your launch site is just past the last of these and before the town pier.

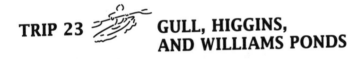

TRIP 23　　GULL, HIGGINS, AND WILLIAMS PONDS

Length: 2 miles

Highlights

This short and easy tour, a favorite with kayakers and canoers, explores three of Wellfleet's more-than-a-dozen kettle ponds, which with a fourth form the source of the Herring River. As you go from pond to pond, you leave human activity behind and instead focus on the natural world, a wonderful arena where plants and animals are the dominant players.

Nearby attractions

The Atlantic White Cedar Swamp, east of Rt. 6 at the end of Marconi Station Rd. in South Wellfleet, has a short, self-guiding nature trail into a former kettle pond that now contains stands of Atlantic white cedar. Across the parking area from the trailhead is the site where in 1903 Guglielmo Marconi sent the first trans-Atlantic wireless message, a greeting from President Theodore Roosevelt to England's King Edward VII.

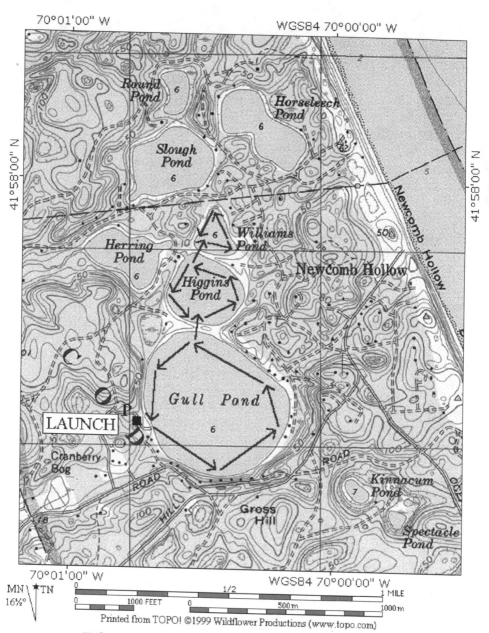

Trip 23—Gull, Higgins, and Williams Ponds

Tips

In summer, paddle in the early morning or the early evening to avoid the crowds and the parking restrictions.

Directions

From Rt. 6 in Wellfleet, north of town, turn east on Gull Pond Rd. just opposite Moby Dick's restaurant. Go 1.1 miles to Schoolhouse Hill Rd. (not signed) and turn left at the stone pillar signed for Gull Pond Landing. At 0.3 mile Schoolhouse Hill Rd. veers left, but you continue straight a few hundred feet and then turn right into a parking area. Continue for several hundred feet to a boat-launching area on your left.

Parking and facilities

A resident parking sticker is required from the last weekend in June through Labor Day, 9 A.M. to 4 P.M. There are rest rooms and picnic tables here.

Launch

From the beach just right of the swimming area.

Trip Description

Cape Cod is famous for its hundreds of kettle ponds, water-filled depressions created by the melting of huge chunks of buried ice left behind as the ice-age glaciers retreated. Some say Wellfleet has the most beautiful of these ponds, and it certainly is graced by a large number of them. There are more than a dozen named ponds within the town's borders, and most of these are on Cape Cod National Seashore land, affording them protection from development. All but a few are on the east side of Rt. 6 in the pine-and-oak woodlands that stretch almost to the Atlantic shore. The largest is Gull Pond at 109 acres and with a maximum depth of 64 feet. Along with its neighbors Higgins, Williams, and Herring ponds, Gull Pond contributes water to the Herring River, a stream that empties into Wellfleet Harbor near Great Island (see previous trip).

As you paddle away from the launch site and turn right, you leave the public beach, crowded and noisy with the shouts of excited children in summer, and begin a counterclockwise circuit past a secluded shoreline and homes tucked away in the pines. Lily pads float just offshore, anchored by long stalks to rhizomes, or roots, buried in the mucky bottom. Because kettle ponds depend on rainwater and groundwater to replenish what they lose through evaporation, recent climatic conditions determine how full or depleted they are. Kettle ponds are fragile ecosystems, and human activity takes its toll on their health and purity. The national seashore has been instrumental in educating the public about how to preserve and protect our kettle ponds and has adopted regulations to insure their survival, such as a ban on the use of soap and shampoo in the ponds and seasonal closures for dogs and other pets.

This pond takes its name from the congregation of gulls usually seen floating in its middle. Other common Cape birds, including cormorants, crows, and bluejays, may also be found here. Stocked with trout, Gull Pond also contains bass, pickerel, yellow perch, and pumpkin-seed sunfish. Paddling parallel to the shoreline, you soon pass a colony of homes on the pond's northeast side, where you may see an array of canoes and kayaks drawn up on shore and a few small sailboats moored just off. Because of the pond's large size, a stiff breeze can roil the waters and even kick up small waves and white caps. As you proceed, the hills on your right gradually dip down until there is only a low, sandy barrier separating Gull Pond from Higgins Pond, its neighbor to the north. A narrow passage, or sluice, cuts through this barrier and lets water move between the ponds. If it has been a rainy winter and spring, the ponds will be full and you may be able to paddle between them. Otherwise you will need to land, get out of your boat, and drag it 100 feet or so over soft sand to Higgins Pond.

This short shore excursion gives you an opportunity to study some of the Cape's common trees and shrubs. Growing here are black oak, scrub oak, smooth alder, bayberry, and poison ivy ("leaves of three, let it be"). Once you

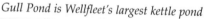

Gull Pond is Wellfleet's largest kettle pond

are back in your boat, you turn right to begin a counterclockwise tour of this pond, which is much smaller and more secluded than its neighbor to the south. In addition to white water lilies, you may find bullhead lilies sporting yellow flowers in summer, and a margin of rushes along the shoreline. Also growing here is pickerelweed, a freshwater plant with arrowhead-shaped leaves and spikes of purple flowers. Your arrival may be noted by a pair of ospreys, large raptors that feed on fish and make their nests near freshwater or saltwater. Hunting also on the wing here may be swallows, darting low over the water to intercept insects. Soon you reach the pond's north shore, where a very narrow cut leads to Williams Pond. This is a shallow passage, so remember to pull up your rudder as you paddle through it. Red maple, tupelo, and sweet pepperbush form a corridor of greenery here, giving cover to nesting birds that may complain about your intrusion.

Williams Pond is the most secluded of the three on this tour—paradise found. It was in a house overlooking this pond that Thoreau spent the night with John Newcomb, a Wellfleet oysterman, and gathered material for one of the best chapters in *Cape Cod*. Here the pond margin is thick with water willow, a vine-like plant with lance-shaped leaves in whorls and, in summer, pink flowers. Marsh ferns along the shore add to the swamp-like atmosphere, and you may be serenaded by a chorus of green frogs, bullfrogs, and Fowler's toads. The tall trees on the pond's east shore are black locust, a fast-growing non-native species that has been planted extensively on the Cape. Unfortunately locusts, having shallow roots, are unable to withstand high winds, making them a liability during hurricanes. Also growing beside the pond is a beautiful stand of willows with long, serrated leaves and drooping catkins. Partially submerged stumps and logs may be occupied by painted turtles taking advantage of sunshine and seclusion. Clumps of blue iris may add a dash of color to the scene. When you have finished enjoying this relaxing, peaceful place, continue around the pond and then paddle back through the cut to Higgins Pond.

Continuing in a counterclockwise direction, you skirt an overgrown cove, right, where a hidden passage leads to Herring Pond and the Herring River. Before the national seashore was instituted, town of Wellfleet crews used to clear brush along the Herring River for mosquito control. In those days it was possible to paddle upstream from near the mouth of the river all the way to the ponds at its source. The river is totally overgrown now, and such a journey would be an act of masochism at best. Now reaching the sluice to Gull Pond, you paddle along its west shore, staying clear of lily pads in shallow water to your right. When you approach the swimming area, marked by ropes, floats, and a raft, use caution and stay clear until you are past it, then turn right to the launch site.

TRIP 24   LIEUTENANT ISLAND AND BLACKFISH CREEK

Length: 6 miles

Highlights

This adventurous and scenic route combines a circuit of Lieutenant Island on the east side of Wellfleet Harbor with an out-and-back exploration of Blackfish Creek, a tidal waterway in a large salt marsh adjacent to Rt. 6. Nesting osprey, terns, and shorebirds may be spotted in season along the way, and you will have an opportunity to practice your route-finding skills as you search for the passage from the harbor under the island's bridge and into Loagy Bay.

Nearby attractions

Massachusetts Audubon Society's Wellfleet Bay Wildlife Sanctuary, located in South Wellfleet west of Rt. 6 near West Rd., is one of the area's premier nature preserves, with hiking trails, guided walks, classes for adults and children, and a beautiful visitor center containing exhibits, books, and helpful staff; (508) 349-2615.

Tips

When you reach the bridge just east of Lieutenant Island, pull off the road and study the tidal creeks to the south. The creek that flows under the bridge divides into two branches, one heading southwest, the other southeast. Coming from the launch site, you will be looking for the southwest channel. The roadway west of the bridge is over low ground that floods at high tide, especially around the times of the full and new moons. During these times, plan to arrive several hours before high tide for Wellfleet Harbor. At other times, launch about one hour before high tide. Avoid hot and humid midsummer days, when there may be swarms of biting greenhead flies. Bring insect repellent to ward off gnats and mosquitoes. When the wind is brisk from the north or east, choose another route.

Directions

From Rt. 6 in Wellfleet, about 1.5 miles north of the Wellfleet/Eastham line and 0.4 mile south of the traffic signal at Marconi Station Rd., turn southwest onto Lieutenant Island Rd. At 1.1 miles you reach a bridge just east of

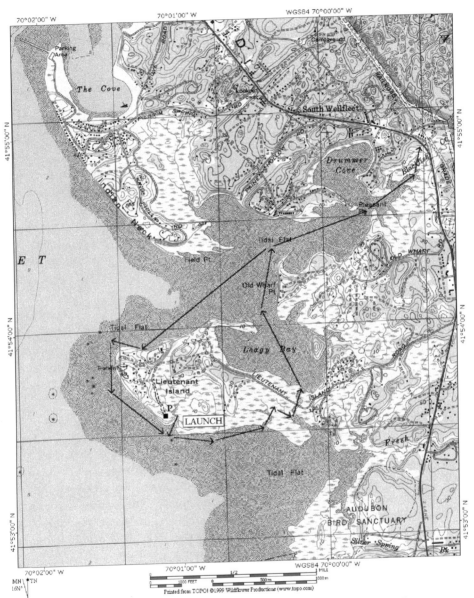

Trip 24—Lieutenant Island and Blackfish Creek

Lieutenant Island. At 1.5 miles the road turns from pavement to dirt with lots of potholes. At 2.1 miles, with a salt marsh on your left, you come to a fork. Veer left and go 0.3 mile to a wide sandy area used for parking. This is an unofficial parking area, and may not be available in the future (see below).

If the parking area above is closed, return to Rt. 6, turn left, and go about 2.5 miles to Pilgrim Spring Rd., just past the fire-lookout tower. Turn left and go about 0.7 mile to a junction where Cove Rd. joins from the right and Indian Neck Rd. goes straight. Go straight 1.8 miles to an intersection with Samoset Ave., left. Here Indian Neck Rd. swings right, and immediately on the left there is a small parking area for Burton Baker Beach. If it is full, continue another 0.3 mile on Indian Neck Rd. to a parking area for Indian Neck Beach.

To reach the route described below from these parking areas, launch into Wellfleet Harbor from either Burton Baker or Indian Neck beach. Turn left, and on a heading of about 170 degrees paddle parallel to the shore of Indian Neck until you are just west of Field Point. Now turn left around the point on a heading of about 100 degrees and join the route just north of Old Wharf Point.

Parking and facilities

There is soft sand just east of the parking area so don't try to drive closer to the water. The parking area may flood at high tide so you may want to move your car to higher ground nearby after unloading your boat. At the alternate parking areas (see above) a permit is required from the last week-end in June through Labor Day.

Launch

In the tidal creek about 400 feet east of the parking area.

Trip Description

This part of Lieutenant Island is owned by the Wellfleet Bay Wildlife Sanctuary, the Cape's premier nature center, which has most of its holdings on the mainland to the southeast. After dragging or carrying your boat to a tidal creek east of the parking area, launch and paddle downstream to the open water, part of Wellfleet Harbor, south of Lieutenant Island. With an osprey-nesting platform on your left and a popular beach on your right, you negotiate shallow water over a sandbar at the mouth of the creek and then turn left. Skirting the edge of a salt marsh, left, you have the wildlife sanctuary across the wide, shallow bay to the southeast. A low, tree-covered rise there is named Try Island after the cauldrons, called try-pots, used to melt whale blubber into oil. Wellfleet was one of New England's first whaling areas, with a steady supply of pilot whales, or blackfish, coming into the harbor's shallow waters mostly during fall and winter. By the mid-18th century, however, shore-whaling, as it was known, had depleted local stocks, and whalemen had to range farther and farther afield. Thus was the whaling industry, whose centers later moved to New Bedford and Nantucket, born.

Schools of pilot whales still occasionally come into the harbor and strand themselves, sparking all-out rescue efforts.

On a heading of about 120 degrees, perhaps aided by a following breeze, you paddle past a tidal creek, left, and then reach a large salt marsh with shallow water and a number of relatively deep channels running through it. Among the birds that frequent this area are gulls, including such common ones as great black-backed, herring, and laughing. A dozen or so species of gulls have been spotted on Cape Cod, along with 11 species of terns, nearly all the species of terns available to most North American birders. With the bridge to Lieutenant Island in sight, turn left into the first deep channel, and when you are within several hundred yards of Lieutenant Island Rd., turn right and paddle parallel to it on a heading of about 130 degrees. This soon brings you to the main creek that flows under the bridge. When you can see a clear passage to the bridge, turn left and paddle under it, ducking if the water is high and shipping your paddle to fit between closely spaced pilings.

Once past the bridge several channels await. Choose the left one and work your way past salt-marsh islands on a heading of almost due north. You soon reach Loagy Bay and make directly north across it for Old Wharf Point. Another osprey-nesting platform is left at about 10 o'clock on a sand spit jutting east from Lieutenant Island. Passing a sandy beach, right, where boats may be moored just offshore, you soon round Old Wharf Point and then turn right and head northeast toward Blackfish Creek, one of Wellfleet's three

Falling tide can leave a kayak high and dry

original harbors. Paddling along the north shore of a wide bay, you follow a heading of about 90 degrees which will carry you to Pleasant Point, a finger of land guarding Drummer Cove. Just behind the shoreline on low, sandy hills carpeted with bearberry are almost-pure stands of pitch pine, which elsewhere on the outer Cape are being infiltrated by deciduous trees such as oak and red maple, a natural process called forest succession. Once past Drummer Cove you enter the wide mouth of Blackfish Creek, a typical tidal stream flowing through a salt marsh.

At high tide the marsh is flooded and the creek runs full, allowing you to paddle all the way to Rt. 6, meeting it just where it makes a sharp westward curve on its way through South Wellfleet. Here the upraised forearm of the Cape is at its narrowest, and only about 1 mile of pine-studded uplands separates Blackfish Creek from the Atlantic Ocean. In fact, visitors to the Marconi Site in Cape Cod National Seashore may be watching you through their binoculars as they stand on the lookout platform there. Beside the creek grow saltwater cordgrass and salt hay, two of the Cape's typical salt-marsh plants. Salt hay, a grass growing in the upper elevations of a salt marsh, was used by Cape farmers as a substitute for the real thing, harvesting it and then feeding it to their cattle and using it to thatch their roofs. Shifting to a heading of about 70 degrees, you penetrate deeper into the marsh, where branching channels lead in various directions. The blue wooden boxes on legs in the marsh are traps for biting flies called greenheads, which make their appearance in midsummer and are particularly annoying on hot and humid days.

Soon the creek begins a series of S-bends and the water gets very murky. If you stay in the middle of the marsh you can follow the main channel all the way to Rt. 6, where the creek widens to form a pool. Along its muddy banks you may see hundreds of male fiddler crabs standing beside their burrows, waving their claws to attract mates and to ward off competitors. As you pass by they will scuttle furiously into their burrows. After you have finished exploring Blackfish Creek, turn around and retrace your route to Old Wharf Point, using a heading of about 270 degrees after you leave the creek. With Old Wharf Point on your left you pass through an area where boats may be moored and then paddle parallel to the north shore of Lieutenant Island, where there are inviting beaches in case you want to land and get out of your boat. To reach them, shift your heading left to about 240 degrees. Field Point and Indian Neck, whose high bluffs are dotted with some fantastic homes, are on your right.

Shallow water along Lieutenant Island's north shore makes for easy landing, but if the tide is dropping don't tarry too long or you will have to drag your boat to launch again. Now you continue counterclockwise around the island, soon reaching a sandy point on its northwest corner where you may spot terns and piping plovers. Once round the point you are in Wellfleet Harbor, with Great Beach Hill and Jeremy Point to the west and one of Wellfleet's popular swimming areas, Mayo Beach, to the north. Turning left, you stay just offshore, and on a summer afternoon you may find yourself beating into a southwest breeze coming across the open water ahead. The island's high point, 60 feet, is just left, atop steep bluffs held in place by riprap. Labeled "Blackfish" on the USGS map, it likely was one of many such elevated places scattered around the harbor that served as lookout points for shore-whalers who hunted pilot whales, or blackfish, in shallow water. Paddling southeast, you soon reach the mouth of the tidal creek where you launched.

Chapter 15

Yarmouth

TRIP 25  LEWIS BAY AND GREAT ISLAND

Length: 6.5 miles

Highlights

This varied out-and-back route explores the north side of Great Island, one of the two enclosing arms that embrace Lewis Bay. Along the way you will paddle past deserted beaches that front forests of eastern red cedar and black oak. Also on the itinerary are several coves and tidal creeks fringed with salt marsh. The sandy beach along Smiths Point offers fine swimming and picnicking, but please observe all posted restrictions to protect nesting terns and piping plovers.

Nearby attractions

Grays Beach, also called Bass Hole Beach, at the end of Centre St. off Rt. 6A in Yarmouthport, has a boardwalk and a trail through a salt marsh at the edge of Cape Cod Bay, great for birding. The Historical Society of Old Yarmouth's Botanic Trails, off Rt. 6A in Yarmouthport, feature native Cape plants on a self-guiding tour. Nearby are two historic houses, the Captain Bangs Hallet House, (508) 362-3021, and the Winslow Crocker House, (508) 362-4385, which display antiques from the 17th to 19th centuries.

Tips

Launch several hours before high tide for Nantucket Sound.

Trip 25—Lewis Bay and Great Island

Directions

From Rt. 6 in Yarmouth take Exit 7, signed for Willow St., Yarmouthport, and W. Yarmouth. Just south on Willow St. is Higgins Crowell Rd., where you turn left. Go 2.6 miles to a traffic signal at Rt. 28. Continue straight, now on Berry Ave. Go 0.7 mile, turn right onto Hampshire Ave., and go about 100 yards to a parking area for Englewood Beach and a boat ramp, left.

Parking and facilities

There is a large parking area here, along with rest rooms, telephone, and soft-drink machine.

Launch

From the boat ramp or, if uncrowded, from the sandy beach just to its left.

Trip Description

Cape Cod has two Great Islands, similar in that they are not true islands, being instead joined to the mainland by tombolos, but different in most other respects. The one in Wellfleet is part of Cape Cod National Seashore, wild and undeveloped, where hikers and boaters are visitors who do not remain. The Great Island that juts southwest from Yarmouth into Nantucket Sound and encloses Lewis Bay is a private gated community reserved for its residents. It too is endowed with great natural beauty and by kayak is the ideal way to

Launching a kayak is easy from Englewood Beach, Lewis Bay

enjoy it: there are shores, scenic inlets, coves, and creeks worth exploring. As you leave the launch site at Englewood Beach you are in a small cove with a swimming beach on your left and a marina with a rock jetty on your right. This cove is a boat moorage for powerboats and sailboats, and you will thread your way among them. Along the shore, left, are classic Cape homes with gray, weathered shingles. Turning left, you paddle parallel to the shoreline, and as it swings south so do you.

On a heading of almost due south, ahead is Pine Island, which sits just north of the sandy strand, or tombolo, that joins Great Island to the mainland. Behind Pine Island is a narrow waterway called Pine Island Creek, which you will explore on the return part of the route. The water just off the mouth of the creek is deep, but the creek's entrance is blocked by a sandbar except at high tide. Across Lewis Bay at about 3 o'clock is Dunbar Point, which with Smiths Point on Great Island guards the entrance from Nantucket Sound to Lewis Bay. On the northwest corner of the bay lies Hyannis Inner Harbor, a busy port that is home to the Martha's Vineyard and Nantucket ferries. As the ferries and other large craft approach the entrance to Lewis Bay they stay in a channel that hugs Dunbar Point. Their wakes, combined with swells sweeping in from the sound, can cause tricky conditions along the west side of Smiths Point.

Catboat plies waters of Nantucket Sound

Turning right and paddling along the north side of Pine Island on a heading of about 310 degrees, you find yourself now in shallow water, perhaps having to steer clear of shellfishing rigs marked by floats. Pine Island is low, sandy, and dotted with stunted trees and scrub vegetation. Soon you pass a second entrance to Pine Island Creek and then a rock jetty at Cedar Point. Left is Great Island, forested here with beautiful stands of eastern red cedar and black oak. Also growing near shore are beach pea, honeysuckle, and black cherry. Raptors may use the tall trees here as perches, so be alert for any frenzied behavior by flocks of shorebirds or terns, often a clue that a hunter is aloft and on the prowl.

As you leave the jetty and the mouth of Pine Island Creek behind, the shoreline swings to the southwest but you stay well offshore to avoid rocks shown on the USGS map. Passing the entrance to Uncle Roberts Cove, where an osprey-nesting platform stands tall, you pass south of Egg Island, a low-lying sandbar that juts northwest from just off Smiths Point. If the island is above water or only slightly awash, gulls and cormorants may be roosting on it. Far to your right rises the white steeple of The Federated Church on Main St. in Hyannis. Now close to Smiths Point, you find deep water as you skirt the south tip of Egg Island. Ahead are a small cove and an open stretch of sandy beach, both inviting places to land. (The area off Smiths Point shown on the USGS map as a tidal flat is now a sand spit.) Here you may find terns and plovers, their nesting areas roped off for protection, and also flocks of Canada geese. Adventurous paddlers may want to continue around Smiths Point and down the west shore of Great Island, but should use caution when close to the main channel: it is the smaller, high-speed ferries on their outbound runs that cause the biggest wakes.

Once you have finished enjoying the waters around Smiths Point, retrace your route to the passage between it and Egg Island, then hug the shoreline—posted as private—until you reach the mouth of Uncle Roberts Cove, guarded by a rock jetty. You turn right, skirting the jetty and then a sandbar poking out from shore, until you are in a lovely, protected cove used as a boat moorage for residents of Great Island, with a small marina on its southwest edge. On the south side of the cove, a tidal creek winds its way under a low bridge that carries one of the island's few roads and continues south through a marsh almost all the way to Nantucket Sound. When you have finished poking around in Uncle Roberts Cove, retrace your route to its entrance, then hug the shoreline back to Cedar Point, aiming for the jetty at the entrance to Pine Island Creek. Keep a sharp eye out for submerged rocks and shellfishing rigs close to shore. Once past the jetty you turn right into Pine Island Creek, here a narrow inlet.

After several hundred yards you come to a **T**-junction. Left is the creek, and right is a circular salt pond, bordered by salt marsh and with a small island in its middle. Here you may find foraging shorebirds such as least sandpipers, probing with their bills for food in the damp mud. After dallying here for a while, paddle east in lovely Pine Island Creek, with Pine Island on your left. Depending on the tide, when you reach the mouth of the creek you may be able to paddle or propel yourself with your hands over the sandbar at its entrance. Otherwise you will have to exit your boat and drag it a few feet to deeper water. Now heading north, retrace your route to the launch site at Englewood Beach, being careful not to stray too far west.

Appendix 1—Selected Reading

Cape Cod

Beston, Henry, *The Outermost House.* New York: Henry Holt and Company, 1992.

Finch, Robert, *Cape Cod: Its Natural and Cultural History.* Washington, DC: National Park Service, 1993.

Finch, Robert, *Common Ground.* Boston: David R. Godine, 1981.

Grant, Kim, *Cape Cod, Martha's Vineyard & Nantucket: An Explorer's Guide.* 3rd ed. Woodstock, VT: The Countryman Press, 1999.

Green, Eugene, and William Sachse, *Names of the Land.* Chester, CT: The Globe Pequot Press, 1983 (out of print).

Hay, John, *The Great Beach.* New York: W. W. Norton & Company, 1980.

Kittredge, Henry C., *Cape Cod: Its People And Their History.* 2nd ed. Hyannis, MA: Parnassus Imprints, Inc., 1987.

Richardson, Wyman, *The House on Nauset Marsh.* Woodstock, VT: The Countryman Press, 1997.

Sabin, Shirley C., and Michael E. Whatley, eds., *Visitor's Guide to Cape Cod National Seashore.* Eastham, MA: Eastern National, 1999.

Thoreau, Henry D., *Cape Cod.* Orleans, MA: Parnassus Imprints, 1984.

Natural History

Berrill, Michael, and Deborah Berrill, *The North Atlantic Coast.* San Francisco: Sierra Club Books, 1981.

Buckley, Ann, and Theodore O. Hendrickson, *Native Trees, Shrubs and Woody Vines of Cape Cod and The Islands.* Dartmouth: University of Massachusetts, 1996.

Dickenson, Mary B., ed., *Field Guide to the Birds of North America.* 3rd ed. Washington, DC: National Geographic Society, 1999.

Flock, Gretchen, and Ann Prince Hecker, eds., *Birding Cape Cod.* South Wellfleet, MA: Massachusetts Audubon Society, 1990.

Hinds, Harold R., and Wilfred A. Hathaway, *Wildflowers of Cape Cod.* Chatham, MA: The Chatham Press, 1968.

Petry, Loren C., and Marcia G. Norman, *A Beachcomber's Botany.* Chatham, MA: The Chatham Conservation Foundation, 1968.

Sterling, Dorothy, *The Outer Lands.* Revised ed. New York: W. W. Norton & Company, 1978.

Strahler, Arthur N., *A Geologist's View of Cape Cod.* Garden City: The Natural History Press, 1966.

Svenson, Henry K., and Robert W. Pyle, *The Flora of Cape Cod*. Brewster, MA: The Cape Cod Museum of Natural History, 1979.

Tiner Jr., Ralph W., *A Field Guide to Coastal Wetland Plants of the Northeastern United States*. Amherst: The University of Massachusetts Press, 1987.

Whatley, Michael E., *Common Trailside Plants of Cape Cod National Seashore*. Eastham, MA: Eastern National, 1988.

Other

Washburne, Randel, *The Coastal Kayaker's Manual*. 2nd ed. Old Saybrook, CT: The Globe Pequot Press, 1993.

Appendix 2—Information Sources

Bird Watchers' General Store, 36 Rt. 6A, Orleans, MA 02653, (508) 255-6974; *Natural History Hotline*, (508) 349-9464

Cape Cod Chamber of Commerce, PO Box 790, Hyannis, MA 02601, (508) 862-0700, (888) 332-2732

Cape Cod Museum of Natural History, Rt. 6A, W. Brewster, MA 02631, (508) 896-3867

Cape Cod National Seashore:
Headquarters, 99 Marconi Site Rd., Wellfleet, MA 02667, (508) 349-3785;
Province Lands visitor center, Race Point Rd., Provincetown, MA 02657, (508) 487-1256;
Salt Pond visitor center, US Highway 6, Eastham, MA 02642, (508) 255-3421

Eastern Mountain Sports, 1513 Iyannough Rd., Hyannis, MA 02601, (508) 362-8690

Eric Gustafson—Fun Seekers, Wellfleet, MA 02667, (508) 349-1429

Goose Hummock Outdoor Center, Rt. 6A, Orleans, MA 02653, (508) 255-2620

Jack's Boat Rentals, Rt. 6, Wellfleet, MA 02667, (508) 349-9808;
on Gull Pond, Wellfleet (508) 349-7553;
on Flax Pond, Nickerson State Park (508) 896-8556

Off the Coast Kayak, 3 Freeman St., Provincetown, MA 02657, (508) 487-2692

The Paddler's Shop, Shipyard Lane, Red Brook Harbor, Cataumet, MA 02534, (508) 563-1784

Waquoit Bay National Estuarine Research Reserve, PO Box 3092. Waquoit, MA 02536, (508) 457-0495;
Washburn Island camping, (877) 422-6762

Waquoit Kayak Co., 1209 E. Falmouth Hwy. (Rt. 28), E. Falmouth, MA 02536, (508) 548-2216, (508) 548-9722

Wellfleet Bay Wildlife Sanctuary, PO Box 236, South Wellfleet, MA 02663, (508) 349-2615

About the Author

Author and professional photographer **David Weintraub** is a resident of San Francisco and has enjoyed the Bay Area's natural beauty for years. Since the early 1950's he has spent summers in Wellfleet on Cape Cod. He is an avid hiker, skier, and kayaker.

His photographs have been published in many books and magazines, including Audubon, Backpacker, Sierra, Smithsonian, and Sunset. His books *East Bay Trails* and *North Bay Trails* are best-selling guides to San Francisco Bay Area hiking.

Index

Kayaking on open water entails unavoidable risk that every kayaker assumes and must be aware of and respect. The fact that a trip is described in this book is not a representation that it will be safe for you. Kayaking trips vary greatly in difficulty and in the degree of conditioning and skill one needs to enjoy them safely. On some trips the area may have changed or conditions may have deteriorated since the descriptions were written. Trip conditions change even from day to day, owing to weather and other factors. A trip that is safe on a calm day or for a highly conditioned, experienced, properly equipped kayaker may be completely unsafe for someone else or unsafe under adverse weather conditions.

You can minimize your risks on the water by being knowledgeable, prepared and alert. There is not space in this book for a general treatise on safety on the water, but there are a number of good books and instruction courses on the subject and you should take advantage of them to increase your knowledge. Just as important, you should always be aware of your own limitations and of conditions existing when and where you are kayaking. If conditions are dangerous, or if you're not prepared to deal with them safely, choose a different trip, or don't go at all. It's better to have wasted a drive than to be the subject of a rescue. These warnings are not intended to scare you off the water. However, one element of the beauty, freedom and excitement of kayaking is the presence of risks that do not confront us at home. When you kayak you assume those risks. They can be met safely, but only if you exercise your own independent judgement and common sense. The author and the publisher of this book disclaim any liability or loss resulting from the use of this book.